The Drug
Legalization
Debate

Second Edition

D060118b

The Drug

Legalization

Debate

Second Edition

James A. Inciardi
Editor

Sage Publications, Inc.
International Educational and Professional Publisher
Thousand Oaks ■ London ■ New Delhi

For information:

Sage Publications, Inc.
2455 Teller Road
Thousand Oaks, California 91320
E-mail: order@sagepub.com

Sage Publications Ltd.
6 Bonhill Street
London EC2A 4PU
United Kingdom

Sage Publications India Pvt. Ltd.
M-32 Market
Greater Kailash I
New Delhi 110 048 India

Printed in the United States of America

Library of Congress Cataloging-in-Publication Data

Main entry under title:

The drug legalization debate / [edited by] James A. Inciardi.—2nd ed.
   p.   cm.
Includes bibliographical references and index.
ISBN 0-7619-0689-4 (cloth: alk. paper)
ISBN 0-7619-0690-8 (pbk.: alk. paper)
   1. Drug legalization—United States.   I. Inciardi, James A.
HV5825 .D7767   1999
363.45′0973—dc21   99-6352

This book is printed on acid-free paper.

99   00   01   02   03   04   05   7   6   5   4   3   2   1

Acquiring Editor: Kassie Gavrilis
Editorial Assistant: Pat Mayer
Production Editor: Astrid Virding
Editorial Assistant: Nevair Kabakian
Typesetter: Lynn Miyata
Indexer: Cristina Haley
Cover Designer: Candice Harman

Contents

1. American Drug Policy: The Continuing Debate   1

   James A. Inciardi

2. Alternative Perspectives on the Drug Policy Debate   9

   Duane C. McBride, Yvonne M. Terry,
   and James A. Inciardi

3. Legalizing Drugs: Would It Really Reduce
   Violent Crime?   55

   James A. Inciardi

4. The Marijuana Legalization Debate:
   Is There a Middle Ground?   75

   Michael L. Dennis and William White

5. **Cannabis, The Wonder Drug**   101
   Lester Grinspoon

6. **Thinking About the Drug Policy Debate**   111
   Erich Goode

7. **Why the Drug War Will Never End**   125
   Steven Jonas

8. **War Is Still Not the Answer**   151
   Karst J. Besteman

9. **Commonsense Drug Policy**   157
   Ethan A. Nadelmann

   Index   173

   About the Contributors   183

American Drug Policy

The Continuing Debate

JAMES A. INCIARDI

*C*oncern over the use and abuse of illegal drugs remained critical throughout the 1990s. In fact, regardless of political affiliation and ideology, socioeconomic status and ethnicity, or geographical location and occupational status, most Americans continued to rank "drugs" among the major problems facing the nation for three reasons. The first was *crack*-cocaine and its relation to crime. Although both the use of crack and rates of violent crime had declined somewhat by the middle of the decade, the linkages between "drugs and crime" had long since become fixed in the mind of America. This was exacerbated by a continuing flow of media stories about drug abuse and the escalating numbers of drug-involved offenders coming to the attention of the police, courts, and prisons.

The second issue was the movement of heroin from the inner city to mainstream culture, and in particular, the increased visibility of heroin in popular culture. A number of celebrated rock groups were linked to heroin use, through a member's overdose, arrest, or admis-

1

sion to treatment—Smashing Pumpkins, Red Hot Chili Peppers, and Nirvana to name but a few. Hollywood also played on heroin's popularity in *Trainspotting*, *Pulp Fiction*, and *Basketball Diaries*. There was the fashion industry's promotion of "heroin chic" images in magazines and on television and billboards. And then there was the death of actor River Phoenix from an overdose of heroin (in combination with cocaine and GHB).

Perhaps the most notable issue that kept drugs in the minds of the American population was the rise in drug use among the nation's youth. In 1993, data from the University of Michigan's annual *Monitoring the Future* study found significant increases in the use of certain drugs among high school seniors, 10th graders, and 8th graders. The use of marijuana in the previous year for all three groups had increased, as did the use of cigarettes in the previous 30 days. Other significant increases included inhalant use among 8th graders, LSD use among seniors, and stimulant use among seniors and 10th graders (Johnston, O'Malley, & Bachman, 1996). In the years hence, the *Monitoring the Future* study documented continuing increases in drug use among youths (Johnston et al., 1996; University of Michigan, 1997). Other national survey data reflected similar trends (Centers for Disease Control [CDC], 1998; Department of Health and Human Services [DHHS], 1998), and regional surveys of adolescent drug use tended to parallel the national trends (for example, see Martin et al., 1997; Terry & Pellens, 1998).

Throughout the 1990s, furthermore, both politicians and the public at large examined American drug policy, pondered its problematic effectiveness, and considered alternatives. New "solutions" were advocated, ranging from mandatory treatment for *all* drug-involved offenders and massive funding for anti-drug media messages, to legalizing some or all drugs of abuse. Within the context of these concerns, assessments, and proposals, it is the intention of this opening commentary to briefly review the American drug experience and to present the backdrop for the modern drug legalization debate.

◼ The American Drug Experience

Drug abuse in the United States evolved within the broader context of the historical relationship between people and the psychoactive organic compounds in their immediate environments. Historians and archaeologists have noted that the use of alcohol is, for the most part, a human cultural universal. The chewing of coca and other psychoactive plants has existed in many societies for millennia. Marijuana and the opium poppy are indigenous to several regions of the world and have been used as intoxicants and in rituals likely since prehistoric times. The explosion of world trade following the European discovery of America brought local psychoactive plants—from tobacco and marijuana to coca and the opium poppy, and related techniques of distillation, refining, and crossbreeding—to the attention of world consumers. The American drug experience emerged, evolved, and endured within the framework of this worldwide trafficking of what was originally local psychopharmacological plants (see Courtwright, 1982; Inciardi, 1986, pp. 1-47; Terry & Pellens, 1928, pp. 53-60).

It began with the widespread use of opium in home remedies and over-the-counter patent medicines during the latter part of the 18th century, followed by the discovery of morphine, cocaine, heroin, and hypodermic needles during the ensuing 100-year period. By 1905 there were more than 28,000 pharmaceuticals containing psychoactive drugs readily available throughout the nation, sold in an unrestricted manner by physicians, over-the-counter from apothecaries, grocers, postmasters, and printers, from the tailgates of medicine show wagons as they traveled throughout rural and urban America, and through the mail by newspaper advertisements and catalog sales (Young, 1961, pp. 19-23). Although little data are available as to the number of people dependent on opiates and cocaine during these years, estimates of the addict population at the close of the 19th century ranged as high as 3 million (Morgan, 1974; Terry & Pellens, 1928, pp. 1-20). Regardless of the accuracy of the estimates, addiction had become so visible and widespread that the medical community, the media, and the public at large called for government restrictions on the availability of drugs.

With the passage of state and local anti-drug statutes at the turn of the 20th century, the Pure Food and Drug Act in 1906, the Harrison Narcotics Act in 1914, and subsequent federal and state legislation, combined with the social and economic upheavals of the Great Depression and World War II, as the United States approached mid-century, drug abuse had significantly receded. During the postwar era of expanded world trade, economic growth, and increased urbanization, however, the drug problem grew apace. In the 1950s, heroin addiction emerged in the inner cities at epidemic levels, particularly among youths. In the 1960s, drug abuse expanded from the cities to suburbia. As part of the social revolution of the decade, adolescents and young adults began to *tune in, turn on,* and *drop out* through a whole new catalog of drugs—marijuana, hashish, and LSD, plus newly synthesized prescription analgesics, stimulants, and sedatives. By the 1970s, the psychedelic revolution of the previous decade had run its course, but the heroin epidemic had endured, marijuana consumption continued to increase, cocaine reentered the drug scene after its half-century sojourn in the netherworlds of vice and the *avant-garde,* and Quaaludes and PCP became prominent as the new drugs of the moment. In the 1980s, most of the old drugs remained prominent, while new entries—designer drugs, ecstasy, and crack—staked out positions. In the 1990s, as noted above, heroin reemerged as the popularity of *crack*-cocaine faltered. At the same time, the use of *powder*-cocaine and other illegal drugs endured, and marijuana and tobacco use increased among youths.

■ America's "War on Drugs"

Since the passage of the Harrison Act in 1914, the federal approach to drug abuse control has included a variety of avenues for reducing both the supply of, and the demand for, illicit drugs. At first, the supply-and-demand reduction strategies were grounded in the classic deterrence model: Through legislation and criminal penalties, individuals would be discouraged from using drugs; by setting an example of traffickers, the government could force potential dealers to seek out other economic pursuits. In time, other components were added: treatment for the user, education and prevention for the would-be user, and research to determine how best to develop and implement plans for enforcement, treatment, education, and prevention.

By the early 1970s, when it appeared that the war on drugs was winning few, if any, battles, new avenues for supply and demand reduction were added. There were the federal interdiction initiatives: Coast Guard, Customs, and Drug Enforcement Administration (DEA) operatives were charged with intercepting drug shipments coming to the United States from foreign ports; in the international sector, there were attempts to eradicate drug-yielding crops at their source. The foreign assistance initiatives also included crop substitution programs and training of Latin American military groups to fight the drug war on their local soil. On the surface, however, none of these strategies seemed to have much effect, and illicit drug use continued to spread.

The problems were many. Legislation and enforcement alone were not enough, and many education programs were of the "scare" variety and quickly lost credibility. Drug abuse treatment was available but not at the level that was needed, and during the 1980s the number of existing treatment slots was drastically reduced. The federal response was, for the most part, a more concerted assault on drugs, both legislative and technological.

By 1988, it had long since been decided by numerous observers that the 74 years of federal prohibition since the passage of the Harrison Act were not only a costly and abject failure but a totally doomed effort as well. It was argued that drug laws and drug enforcement had served mainly to create enormous profits for drug dealers and traffickers, overcrowded jails, police and other government corruption, a distorted foreign policy, predatory street crime carried on by users in search of the funds necessary to purchase black market drugs, and urban areas harassed by street-level drug dealers and terrorized by violent street gangs (McBride, Burgman-Habermehl, Alpert, & Chitwood, 1986; Rosenbaum, 1987; Trebach, 1987; Wisotsky, 1986).

◼ The Drug Legalization Debate

Discussions about legalizing drugs in the United States go back to the early decades of the 20th century. The contemporary debate over the legalization of drugs, however, emerged in 1988. It began at a meeting of the U.S. Conference of Mayors when Baltimore's Kurt L. Schmoke called for a national debate on American drug control strategies and the potential benefits of legalizing marijuana, heroin, cocaine, crack, and other illicit substances. Schmoke's argument was that for generations the United States had been pursuing policies of prosecution and repression that resulted in little more than overcrowded courts and prisons, increased profits for drug traffickers, and higher rates of addiction (Schmoke, 1989).

The drug legalization debate received considerable attention in 1988 and 1989. Media coverage was extensive, and discussions of the futility of the "drug wars" became widespread in many academic circles. In the 1990s, however, the tenor of the drug debate began to change. A number of the more "hard core" legalizers softened their positions somewhat, advocating a "harm reduction" approach in favor of legalization. At the same time, many of those on the other side of the debate continued to oppose legalizing drugs but began to accept several aspects of the harm-reduction approach.

For those new to the drug policy debates, "harm reduction" is a concept that has been difficult to define with any degree of precision. For the most part, however, its essential feature is the attempt to ameliorate the adverse health, social, legal, and/or economic consequences associated with the use of mood-altering drugs. As such, harm reduction is neither a policy nor a program but, rather, a principle which suggests that managing drug misuse is more appropriate than attempting to stop it altogether. Within this context, harm reduction can mean different things to different people, groups, cultures, and nations. Most broadly, it can refer to any variety of policies and policy goals, including the following:

1. *Advocacy for changes in drug policies*—legalization, decriminalization, ending the drug prohibition, reduction of criminal sanctions for drug-related crimes, changes in drug paraphernalia laws

2. *HIV/AIDS-related interventions*—needle/syringe exchange programs, HIV prevention/intervention programs, bleach and condom distribution programs, referrals for HIV and other sexually transmitted disease (STD) testing; referrals for HIV and other STD medical care and management, referrals for HIV/AIDS-related psychological care and case management

3. *Broader drug treatment options*—methadone maintenance by primary care physicians, changes in methadone regulations, heroin substitution programs, new experimental treatments, treatment on demand

4. *Drug abuse management for those who wish to continue using drugs*—counseling and clinical case management programs that promote safer and more responsible drug use

5. *Ancillary interventions*—housing and other entitlements, healing centers, support and advocacy groups (Inciardi & Harrison, in press)

Currently, harm reduction per se is not officially a part of American drug policy, and in fact, the term itself has become so value-laden among many U.S. drug strategists and politicians that it is rarely articulated within government circles. This has occurred, for the most part, because "harm reduction" is often used interchangeably with such expressions as "drug legalization" and "marijuana decriminalization." But as is made clear in several of the chapters in this volume, advocating harm reduction does not necessarily mean promoting the legalization of heroin, cocaine, and other currently illegal drugs. Rather, harm reduction can focus on many different alternatives, including drug abuse education, prevention, and treatment. Within this context, *The Drug Legalization Debate*, 2nd edition addresses the many sides of the legalization/ harm-reduction issue as well as commenting on a variety of policy alternatives.

■ References

Centers for Disease Control. (1998). *Tobacco use among U.S. racial/ethnic minority groups.* Available at http://www.cdc.gov/nccdphp/osh/sgr-min-fs-afr.htm

Courtwright, D. T. (1982). *Dark paradise: Opiate addiction in America before 1940.* Cambridge, MA. Harvard University Press.

Department of Health and Human Services. (1998, August 21). *Annual national drug survey results released: Overall drug use is level, but youth drug increase persists.* Press release: http://www.health.org/pubs/nhsda/97hhs/nhs97rel.htm

Inciardi, J. A. (1986). *The war on drugs: Heroin, cocaine, crime, and public policy.* Palo Alto, CA: Mayfield.

Inciardi, J. A., & Harrison, L. D. (in press). *Harm reduction: National and international perspectives.* Thousand Oaks, CA: Sage.

Johnston, L. D., O'Malley, P. M., & Bachman, J. G. (1996, December 19). *Monitoring the future.* News release, Ann Arbor, University of Michigan.

Martin, S. S., Enev, T. E., Peralta, R. L., Purcell, C. L., Logio, K. A., & Murphy, R. G. (1997). *Alcohol, tobacco, and other drug abuse among Delaware students.* Report to the Delaware Prevention Coalition, University of Delaware.

McBride, D. C., Burgman-Habermehl, C., Alpert, J., & Chitwood, D. D. (1986). Drugs and homicide. *Bulletin of the New York Academy of Medicine, 62,* 487-508.

Morgan, H. W. (1974). *Yesterday's addicts: American society and drug abuse.* Norman: University of Oklahoma Press.

Rosenbaum, R. (1987, February 15). Crack murder: A detective story. *New York Times Magazine*, pp. 24-33, 57, 60.

Schmoke, K. L. (1989). Foreword. *American Behavioral Scientist, 32*(3), 231-232.

Terry, C. E., & Pellens, M. (1928). *The opium problem*. New York: Bureau of Social Hygiene.

Trebach, A. S. (1987). *The great drug war*. New York: Macmillan.

University of Michigan News and Information Services. (1997, December 20). *Drug use among American teens shows some signs of leveling after a long rise*. Press release.

Wisotsky, S. (1986). *Breaking the impasse in the war on drugs*. Westport, CT: Greenwood.

Young, J. H. (1961). *The toadstool millionaires: A social history of patent medicines in America before federal regulation*. Princeton, NJ: Princeton University Press.

2

Alternative Perspectives on the Drug Policy Debate

DUANE C. MCBRIDE
YVONNE M. TERRY
JAMES A. INCIARDI

Although the term "War on Drugs" was first coined by the Nixon Administration in 1970 to 1971, it was not until the Reagan administration in the 1980s that the term became widely used. The designation seemed particularly applicable amidst the era's zero tolerance drug policy and interdiction efforts. As the Reagan administration began, illegal drug use stood at historic highs; it was likely that as many high school seniors were using marijuana annually as tobacco (Johnston, O'Malley, &

9

Bachman, 1997). Large proportions of the youth and young adult populations as well as government officials were calling for the legalization of marijuana (DuPont, 1979). Reactions to these use levels and attitudes toward legalization played a major role in the election of a conservative Republican president and Senate committed to rolling back the high rates of illegal drug abuse and halting the legalization movement. Both the nation and grassroots community movements believed that with enough resources, multi-level efforts and political will, illegal drug use could be virtually eliminated in contemporary society.

The drug war was almost exclusively an interdiction effort. However, philosophical positions other than prohibition have always existed, and they continue to vigorously participate in the drug policy debate. Contributions have come from civil libertarians, public health practitioners, harm reduction supporters, criminal justice punitive paradigm proponents—all representatives of the continuum upon which drug policy travels. Meanwhile, the pendulum of the continuum still hangs over the punitive criminal justice paradigm largely as a result of programs initiated almost 20 years ago during the Reagan administration. Why has this paradigm been so successful among voters and politicians? Should it remain there? Are civil libertarians correct in their claims that the present war is not only a failure but also an unnecessary invasion of the rights guaranteed by the U.S. Constitution? Is the voice of the criminal justice system justified in its assertion that only by punitive measures can American society be kept as safe as possible from the violence and social decay associated with illegal drug use? Should U.S. policy move toward a public health harm reduction position? What role should drug treatment play in the War on Drugs? Are more effective alternative policy positions available?

No brief chapter can provide a sufficient investigation into the complex arguments surrounding the drug policy debate, and possibly the subject will never be neatly and tidily resolved. However, the next few pages attempt to present an overview and background of the drug policy debate together with current arguments and evaluations of various positions.

▓ History and Background

Commercialism

The first national drug policy in the United States could be labeled "commercialism." Nineteenth-century America was characterized by virtually unlimited acceptance of free market distribution of goods and services. No laws existed for regulating type, quality, or effects of products sold (including powerful chemicals). The best illustration of this policy is reflected in the 1904 Sears catalog wherein heroin, barbiturates, and necessary injection paraphernalia were all advertised. The U.S. Public Health Service has estimated that between 1859 and 1899 about 7,000 tons of crude opium and 800 tons of smoking opium were imported into the United States (Kolb & Du Mez, 1924). At the time, the distribution of many drugs was intimately tied into the legitimate economy. It was well-integrated into economic and political systems as well as everyday community life (for a discussion of this era, see Inciardi, 1992; Musto, 1973).

The Early Reform Era

The widespread commercial distribution of addictive chemicals generated significant reaction. Moral reformers decried the use of all intoxicating chemicals as inherently wrong; public health reformers focused on product safety and quality (often calling for full labeling of all ingredients); and the newly developing American Medical Association desired to raise the standards of medical education and control the distribution of medicines under physicians (see Young, 1967). Within this reactionary attitude toward laissez-faire distribution, the law enforcement community also weighed in with a simple solution: Those who used addictive substances were nonproductive, criminal and should be prosecuted. Largely through the moral enterprises of social reformers and the successful attempts of the medical profession during the 1880s and 1890s to control the distribution of drugs, the use of certain substances (initially opium and morphine, followed by cocaine and marijuana) came to be defined as sinful, deviant, outright wicked, and dangerous without the close supervision of a physician (Terry & Pellens, 1928). By the turn of the 20th century, politicians, police and general community members had advanced claims that drug use was linked to the criminal underworld. The 1914 Harrison Act was, on its surface, simply a tax requiring those who distributed certain drugs to obtain a tax stamp. However, the Supreme Court and subsequent federal enforcement agencies (such as the Federal Bureau of Narcotics established in 1930) interpreted the implications of the Act as forbidding any distribution or medical prescription of the listed drugs (e.g., see *United States v. Behrman*, 1922). By the close of the 1930s, policymakers had constructed an image of drug users as "dope fiends" facing a lifetime of slavery to drugs (Inciardi, 1986).

Court and legislative interpretations of the Harrison Act assured the triumph of the criminal justice punitive perspective and zero tolerance policy. While the voices of civil libertarians, public health practitioners and medical professionals remained, few critics of control efforts emerged during the early years of 20th-century drug policy formation. A conspicuous exception in this regard was Alfred R. Lindesmith. During the 1930s, Lindesmith was a graduate student at the University of Chicago and in subsequent years a member of the sociology faculty at Indiana University. Lindesmith's first exposure to the drug field was through criminal addicts, but the majority of his thinking was influenced by his research with patients at the U.S. Public Health Service Hospital in Lexington, Kentucky. At that time, the addict population there was composed of individuals addicted to either morphine or paregoric, and their drugs had been obtained from physicians through either legal or quasi-legal means. They were members of neither the criminal underworld nor street subcultures. Lindesmith argued that criminal penalties were inappropriate for these patients who were suffering from the chronic and relapsing disease of addiction. He concluded that punishment—based on rational choice theory—would be ineffective as a means to stop addiction (Lindesmith, 1938, 1940). Although a direct call for the legalization of drugs was not apparent in Lindesmith's early work, it was clearly implied. His arguments for policy changes were criticized at the federal level (Michelsen, 1940) and then essentially ignored. Between the passage of the Harrison Act and the 1960s, there was little opposition to the dominant law enforcement paradigm. Law enforcement was able to mobilize a considerable breadth of support throughout the 1950s. Even the media cooperated by producing such movies as *Reefer Madness* and *Man with the Golden Arm*. Both of these movies portrayed illegal drug users as hopelessly immoral and dangerous, driven insane by their need for drugs.

Impact of the Baby Boomers

Arguments for changes in drug policy—including perhaps even the legalization of some drugs—came to the forefront during the latter part of the 1960s through the 1970s. The shift occurred probably as the result of the demographic revolution and consequent cultural behavioral change of the young adulthood of the baby boomers (those born between 1946 and 1958). Social scientists have documented that the baby boomers had higher rates of criminal behavior (Cohen & Land, 1987), drug use (Inciardi, McBride, & Surratt, 1998) and behaviors that latter came to be associated with HIV-infection risk (McBride, 1990) than either earlier or subsequent generations. The 1960s and 1970s were a time when drug use seemed to leap from the marginal zones of society to the very center of middle-class community life. By 1975, the majority of high school seniors in the United States admitted to using an illegal drug at least once in their lives. Just under half (45%) reported using an illegal drug in the last year (Johnston et al., 1997). In fact, the majority of high school seniors from 1977 through 1981 self-reported using some form of illegal drug other than alcohol and tobacco at least annually; for the years 1978 and 1979, the majority of high school seniors self-reported smoking marijuana annually. Even at a daily use level, marijuana was used by 9% to 10% of high school seniors from 1977 through 1980. This was a higher daily use rate than alcohol (but only about half the use rate of cigarettes). As the use of heroin, marijuana, and a variety of hallucinogenic drugs increased, so too did the number of arrests on drug charges of apparently otherwise law-abiding citizens (McBride, 1976). Spirited by the liberalism of the era, social science community discussions about drugs often encouraged some form of legalization. It was argued that by legalizing the possession and sale of the whole spectrum of illicit drugs lives would no longer be disrupted by arrests, the drug black market would shrink, and drug-related crime would eventually disappear. In fact, data from the *Monitoring the Future* study showed that about two thirds of the senior class of 1977 and 1978 saw no great risk in regular use of marijuana. Further, about 45% of this class did not see great risk in trying heroin once or twice and only about one fourth of the class believed that private marijuana use should be illegal. Nearly one third of the cohort thought marijuana should be entirely legal (Johnston, O'Malley, & Bachman, 1998).

The establishment of a drug-oriented popular media closely followed these rapid changes in use patterns. The magazine *High Times* regularly advertised marijuana paraphernalia as well as information on use techniques. In addition, the National Organization for Reform of Marijuana Laws (NORML) was initiated to work for the legalization of marijuana. By 1972, the National Commission on Marijuana and Drug Abuse recommended the decriminalization of marijuana. In a February 4, 1979 speech, Dr. Robert DuPont (then director of the National Institute on Drug Abuse, or NIDA) argued, "There are sound reasons for decriminalizing [marijuana]" (DuPont, 1979). DuPont essentially stated that other psychotropic drugs such as alcohol and tobacco were legal and widely distributed by legitimate businesses, so it made no sense to criminalize a substance that was apparently much less harmful than those two already available drugs. He also argued that if legalization had negative consequences, it could always be reversed. Dr. DuPont was the first (and last) NIDA director to call for the legalization of an illegal drug.

In addition to calls for some level of decriminalization, the 1960s and 1970s saw major attempts to reform punitive drug policy by moving toward a mental health perspective. These attempts often drew upon a 1962 Supreme Court ruling concluding that the federal government could not punish drug addicts simply for being addicted (*Robinson v. California*, 1962). One of the consequences of this ruling was later legislation offering treatment instead of criminal processing and imprisonment for illegal drug users. Such legislation took several routes. The Narcotic Addict Rehabilitation Act (NARA) of 1966 focused on sending illegal drug users to federal narcotics hospitals instead of prison by means of diversion and direct commitment in lieu of prosecution. Major diversion programs were initiated that diverted drug users from criminal justice processing into treatment such as the National Treatment Alternatives to Street Crime program (Inciardi & McBride, 1991; McBride & Dalton, 1977). Although many in the mental health community objected and questioned if treatment could be effective with coerced clients, there was evidence that the use of criminal and civil law resulted in increased treatment utilization, retention and effectiveness (see Anglin et al., 1996; Inciardi, McBride, & Rivers, 1996).

The Reagan Era

The years 1979–1981 found illegal drug use among high school students at historic highs. Over 50% of the students in the senior classes of 1979 and 1980 had used marijuana within the past year. In the senior class of 1981, about one third reported use of at least one other illegal drug in the past year (over 20% reported using amphetamines), and over 12% reported at least annual use of cocaine (Johnston et al., 1997). However, the inauguration of President Ronald Reagan in 1981 changed the debate, the direction of national policy, and even federal responsibility for illegal drug use and users. A conservative Congress virtually stopped the national debate about drug legalization and considerably reduced funding for and national interest in federally funded drug treatment. Official policy became "Just Say No"—zero tolerance. Draconian laws were passed during the 1980s requiring mandatory lengthy sentencing for relatively small amounts of cocaine or other drug possession. There were also major efforts on the interdiction front. In fact, with the devolution of authority and interest in local treatment, interdiction and the use of the criminal justice system for punitive treatment of drug users seemed to be the only national policy.

▪ The Beginnings of the Modern Drug Policy Debate

By the close of the 1980s, even proponents of the War on Drugs recognized that society's attitudes toward drug use and actual use patterns had significantly changed. The *Monitoring the Future* study shows that annual illegal drug use among seniors declined from a high of 54% in 1979 to a low of 27% in 1992 (Johnston et al., 1997). However, drug use dramatically increased in other parts of society, particularly among those involved in the criminal justice system. Data collected in the early to mid-1970s generally found less than 20% of those involved with the criminal justice system were current illegal drug users (McBride, 1976). By the 1990s, data showed that a large majority of felony arrestees in major metropolitan areas of the Unites States were currently using an illegal drug, usually cocaine (Arrestee Drug Abuse Monitoring Program, 1998). Beginning in the late 1980s, numerous observers concluded that the 74 years of federal prohibition, the 1980s' effort at zero tolerance, and increased punishments were of very limited success—particularly for the most vulnerable populations—and had major civil rights consequences. Critics argued that drug laws and drug enforcement had served mainly to create enormous profits for drug dealers and traffickers, overcrowded jails, corruption among police and other government employees, a distorted foreign policy, predatory street crime perpetuated by users in search of the funds necessary to purchase black market drugs, and urban areas harassed by street-level drug dealers and terrorized by violent drug gangs (Kraar, 1988; McBride, Burgman-Habermehl, Alpert, & Chitwood, 1986; Morganthau et al., 1988; "Neighbors," 1988; Raab, 1988; Rosenbaum, 1987; "Savage Ride," 1988; Trebach, 1987; Wisotsky, 1986).

Expenditures for the War on Drugs had been considerable. Federal disbursements for supply and demand reduction from 1981 through 1988 totaled some $16.5 billion (Office of Management and Budget with 1988 costs estimated, see Inciardi & McBride, 1990). These figures did not include the many more billions of dollars spent by state and local governments on law enforcement and other criminal justice system costs or on prevention, education, treatment, or research. On the positive side of the equation, interdiction initiatives had also resulted in the seizure of some 5.3 million kilograms of marijuana between 1981 through 1987. More important, cocaine seizures had increased dramatically from 2,000 kilograms in 1981 to almost 60,000 kilograms in 1988 (Inciardi, 1986).

While these figures appeared to be impressive and seemed to indicate a successful interdiction policy, Customs, Coast Guard, and

Drug Enforcement Administration (DEA) officials readily admitted that the seizures probably reflected only about 10% of the marijuana and cocaine entering the country (U.S. General Accounting Office, 1987). Furthermore, DEA figures indicated that despite the seizures and increased expenditures on interdiction, a growing supply and purity of the cocaine entering the United States had resulted in an increased availability coupled with a dramatic decline in price (Rinfret, 1988). This same trend could also be seen in the increased worldwide production of both marijuana and opium (U.S. Department of State, 1988). Meanwhile, many countries seemed unable or unwilling to take a stand against drug traffickers, further exacerbating the constraints of interdiction efforts. Within this context, concerns over the extent and long-term consequences of illegal drug use in the United States was again raised and the closing years of the 1980s witnessed a renewed call for the legalization, if not outright decriminalization, of most or all illicit drugs.

Changing Drug Use Patterns in the 1990s

Current national drug policy debate has also been framed by a significant shift in drug use patterns among youths. Although drug use has stabilized among felony arrestees, there has been a significant change in the prevalence of drug use among the nation's youths and in their attitudes toward use and legalization. From a 1992 annual drug use low of 27% among high school seniors, use prevalence has steadily risen year after year. The senior class of 1997 reported a 42% use rate, an increase of 15 percentage points over the class of 1992. Data from the same classes further showed the greatest increase in the use of marijuana, but also indicated increases in the annual use of every type of drug except alcohol. The increases in the use of illegal drugs was also accompanied by higher rates of tobacco use. Only 17% of the class of 1992 smoked tobacco daily within a 30-day period. In the class of 1997, 25% of the population reported daily tobacco use (Johnston et al., 1997). The increase in use has been accompanied by a steady decrease in the perception of both risk and disapproval of most types of drugs, particularly marijuana. About one fourth of the class of 1992 thought there were great health risks in trying marijuana even one or twice. This perception had apparently decreased to 15% for the class of 1997. Disapproval for experimental marijuana use dropped from 70% for the class of 1992 to 51% for the class of 1997 (Johnston et al., 1997).

These large changes in use patterns and perceived harmfulness have added fuel to the drug policy discussion. Current positions on this issue fall along a continuum ranging from strict punitive prohibition at one end to hands-off, free market decriminalization at the other. However as the following section illustrates, the debate is certainly not limited to only the extremes.

■ The Debate Continuum Today

In an excellent review of the legalization debate, Erich Goode (1997) proposed a useful framework for organizing drug policy discussion in the late 1990s. This chapter uses Goode's work as a framework; however, some modifications have been made and were intended to more clearly differentiate existing positions. As Goode notes, there are two major positions at the core of the debate: continued prohibition and some form of legalization including decriminalization (with considerable variance existing within these positions). As previously alluded to, the various positions can be viewed as points along a continuum of discussion rather than as the adversarial strongholds often portrayed in caricature. Successful policy development will depend on finding points along this continuum that can build consensus versus hard line adherence to particular views. The present discussion of the alternatives moves from the current policy emphasis on prohibition (and its critiques) to middle-ground harm reduction, to medicalization and legalization/regulation policy movements, and then to the more extreme position of total decriminalization. Specifically, the following categories (based on Goode, 1997) are discussed:[1]

■ *Prohibition*—This position is current drug policy. Supporters tend to focus on the necessity for continuing prohibition of the use of illegal drugs through severe penalties for production, distribution, and use.

■ *Harm Reduction*—This approach focuses on using a public health model to reduce the risk and consequences of drug use. Specific program elements include education, prevention and treatment as well as instructing users about how to use drugs more safely. To meet these objectives, provisions may involve the distribution to users of materials such as clean needles or bleach.

- *Medicalization*—This perspective views substance use as a medical issue and emphasizes the role of physicians. Medicalization policy supporters advocate giving physicians sole responsibility to treat drug users, including the decision to maintain drug users on the drug to which they have become addicted.

- *Legalization/Regulation*—This position argues for governmental regulation of currently illegal drugs and often also favors tighter regulations of legal drugs. This approach would consider licensing the distribution of some currently illicit drugs but is often drug specific. That is, some drugs might be decriminalized, some legalized, and some still prohibited.

- *Decriminalization*—This position essentially advocates the complete removal of any legal regulation or penalties for the use of currently illegal substances. Those supporters of this position often call for scientifically accurate drug education but firmly believe that educated, intelligent adults should be free to chose their private behaviors and that an informed public will make reasonable decisions. This position also includes partial decriminalization. That is, only some drugs (most often marijuana) would be decriminalized.

Continuing Prohibition

National policy on drug use and abuse in the United States has been prohibitionist since the early 1900s. As noted, prohibition is rooted in the moral, professional, and social reform movements of the late 19th century. Prohibitionist views are an integral part of American culture and values and retain a significant amount of political power. From a "strict" prohibitionist perspective, alternatives to current policy should emphasize the more consistent application of punitive measures. Those who subscribe to strict prohibition advocate the use of law enforcement with severe penalties, the goal being deterrence and complete elimination of illicit drug use (Goode, 1997). "Moderate" prohibitionists, however, support the logic of relative deterrence: acknowledging that the goal of eliminating illicit drug use is unattainable, moderates believe use of law enforcement is necessary to curtail illicit drug use as much as possible. However, the legislative law would primarily focus on drug production and major distribution. Both strict and moderate viewpoints support continued use of the criminal justice system in the battle against drug use. Although the type and extent of use of the justice system may vary significantly depending on which position is taken by prohibitionists, the basic policy implications for the position are punitive: Primary focus is on the arrest, conviction, prosecution, and incarceration of drug sellers and users (Goode, 1997), followed by support for drug interdiction efforts and demand reduction (prevention and treatment).

The arguments used by prohibition supporters have remained relatively stable over time. In their analysis of the drug legalization debates carried out in the nation's newspapers, MacCoun, Kahan, Gillespie, and Rhee, (1993) show that since the 1970s prohibitionists have primarily argued that moves toward legalization or decriminalization would result in (a) increases in the number of users and addicts and (b) increases in the numbers of drug-related health consequences. Additional concerns raised by those arguing for continued prohibition against legalization or decriminalization include the following (see Kleiman, 1992; McBride, 1995; Ruche, 1995; Stares, 1996a, 1996b; Trebach & Inciardi, 1993):

- Immoral aspects of illicit drug use

- Further disruption of family structure

- Increased public health safety hazards, including risk of AIDS from injection drug use and sex practices associated with drug addiction

- Disproportionate harm to the poor and minorities

- Increased crime due to use and addiction consequences, including economic demands and psychopharmacological consequences

- Implied endorsement of drug use to American youths, thereby lowering perceptions of harm and risk (known deterrents to use)

- Increased school and work problems due to drug-related lack of concentration, desire for achievement, and affected memory

- An overall lack of details on policy implementation suggested by legalization proponents (crucial regulatory questions such as terms of supply and consumption as well as the nature of the product allowed not explained)

- Demonstrated success of prohibition in lowering—while not eliminating—use rates in the general population

■ Current legalization policies (such as the legalization/regulation of alcohol and tobacco) have shown that attempts to use regulation to prevent the selling of these substances to minors are not successful. The free market system of marketing and advertising has obviously overridden governmental attempts to regulate and prevent alcohol and tobacco consumption among youths.

In addition to discussions in the popular press, antilegalization and antidecriminalization viewpoints are supported by various professional organizations as well as by the majority of Americans. The American Medical Association has taken a fairly prohibitive stance calling "for the formulation of a comprehensive national drug policy that recognizes the complexity of drug abuse and prohibits drug legalization" (Voelker, 1997, p. 802). Public opinion polls of Americans show that 90% oppose legalizing the possession and sale of hard drugs and 75% oppose such legislation for marijuana (Goode, 1997). In research conducted with American high school students, 61% to 84% of students feel the use of hard drugs should be prohibited by law, and almost 70% feel public use of marijuana should be prohibited (Johnston ct al., 1998). It is important to recognize that a significant part of national drug policy rests on a broad base of community support. After all, it is not a course of action imposed on the people by an autocratic government but, rather, a policy that reflects the view of the majority as its members consider the marketplace of drug policy ideas.

There are those in the prohibitionist camps who have called for even harsher criminal justice penalties for drug use. Darryl Gates (former Los Angeles Police Department Chief) stated that recreational marijuana users "ought to be taken out and shot" (Beers, 1991, p. 38); William Bennett (former federal drug czar) was quoted as saying that individuals selling illegal drugs to children should be beheaded (Goode, 1997; Lazare, 1990). Hyperbolic utterances aside, these individuals and others appear to believe that penalties must be certain and sufficiently severe if society is to actually achieve the virtual elimination of illegal drug use. Theoretically, those who advocate this position are working under the belief that severity and certainty of punishment are effective in changing and controlling deviant behavior. In a 1994 *Wall Street Journal* article, William Bennett attributed the emerging increases in illegal drug use to a reduction in the severity and certainty of punishment for drug law violations in the Clinton administration. Bennett (1994) noted that Janet Reno favored reduction of mandatory minimum sentences for drug trafficking and that President Clinton reduced the funding of the Office of National Drug Control Policy. Similarly, James Q. Wilson from UCLA argued that harsher penalties for criminal behaviors, including drug use, have played a role in the recent decrease in crime rate and rate of drug use throughout the late 1980s and early 1990s (Wilson, 1994). From this perspective, it is the failure to consistently apply national drug policy that has resulted in the recent increases in illegal drug use.

It should also be noted that current American drug policy exists within a complex series of both international agreements and international law. Many countries have prohibitive laws against specific types of drugs, and in fact, American economic assistance often hinges on an evaluation of a country's enforcement of prohibition policies. As such, the punitive policies of other countries stand as testimony to the fact that prohibitionists are not the only advocates of strict penalties for solving the drug problem. For example, China and other countries that are a part of resurgent Islam have much stricter and certainly what may be considered more draconian punishments for violation of drug laws, including but not limited to the death penalty.

Finally, there are many who view themselves as generally within the prohibitionist tradition yet also believe modifications to existing drug policy are needed. For example, McBride (1995), Falco (1989) and Inciardi (Trebach & Inciardi, 1993) strongly argue for increased federal support of treatment as well as a focus on the basic underlying causes of drug use and the need for improved educational and economic opportunities in at-risk populations.

Critics of Prohibition

Criticisms of the current drug policy are varied, passionate, and come from a wide variety of perspectives. While the various other policy positions presented in this chapter each have specific criticisms of current prohibition policy, they generally focus on the following issues:

- Current policy is not meeting its goals of reducing illegal drug use or its consequences. Demand for illegal drugs has not been reduced in vulnerable populations (such as felony arrestees) or in the general population as evidenced by recent significant increases in illegal drug use among high school seniors.

- The high percentage of illegal drug use among arrestees (particularly cocaine use) indicates that current policy significantly contributes to criminal behavior among drug users. This suggests that drug laws simply criminalize a medical and public health problem and ask the legal system to deal with what it is, in fact, unable to affect: a medical condition.

- The enforcement of drug laws has considerably eroded hard-won civil rights (Duke & Gross, 1994). There have been too many innocent citizens killed or injured by overzealous drug agents in their attempts to enforce draconian drug laws (Fratello, 1994).

- Drug law enforcement is often racist, with African Americans receiving harsher penalties than Whites.

- Current drug policy that forbids the distribution of clean syringes and needles has caused considerable public health harm, including HIV infection and consequent perinatal transmission.

- Drug laws corrupt and overwhelm the criminal justice system. There are simply so many drug cases that criminal courts are overwhelmed. Even the creation of drug courts has not significantly addressed this problem. Illegal drug use rates are so high that society simply cannot arrest, process, and imprison all of the population involved. As a result, drug laws are selectively enforced, causing attendant problems of bias and corruption.

- Finally, the American public appears to be reducing its support of current prohibition policies as evidenced by increasing support for the legalization of marijuana reported in the *Monitoring the Future* study (Johnston et al., 1998) and by recent referendums in California and other states.

Critics from all parts of the debate spectrum call for a recognition that current policy is failing. They ask for a careful review of other options that might more effectively achieve the worthwhile social goals of reducing drug use and all of its personal and criminal consequences while diminishing the high level of collateral damage to bystanders and civil rights that seems to be the payment demanded by current policies. These criticisms and suggested modifications bring the debate away from strict prohibitionist views and into the middle of the drug legalization debate: the harm reduction approach.

Harm Reduction Models

The bottom line in harm reduction models is just that: reducing the harm caused by drug use and abuse by whatever means may be necessary, regardless of how such methods may appear to a conservative public: "The essential feature of harm reduction is the attempt to ameliorate the adverse health, social, or economic consequences associated with the use of mood-altering substances without necessarily requiring a reduction in the consumption of these substances" (Inciardi & Harrison, in press). Supporters of harm reduction-based policy initiatives strike a balance between prohibitionists and decriminalizers: They acknowledge that the current policy is not working and is in need of significant reform, yet they are generally not in favor of full decriminalization. Harm reduction models are a combination of lowered emphasis on the criminal justice system, increased treatment and education, and expansion of services such as needle and condom distribution that reduce the harmful consequences of risk behavior. In essence, a public health preventive model is suggested. As Bertram, Blachman, Sharpe, and Andreas (1996) note, a public health approach would involve fundamentally different questions about policy effectiveness. Instead of looking to interdiction and arrest data to measure progress, American media and political members would be concerned with the following issues (Bertram et al., 1996, p. 204):

- If a particular program attracted substance abusers into treatment
- If a program enabled participants to find or keep jobs
- If the spread of AIDS and other drug-related diseases was slowed as a result of a program

Harm reduction models call for de-emphasizing punitive criminal justice interventions, especially for more trivial offenses such as individual use, possession, and small-scale dealing. Use of the criminal justice system would be focused on large-scale dealers and traffickers of hard drugs such as cocaine and heroin. The criminal justice system would also be involved as a point of intervention emphasizing treatment versus incarceration for drug offenders. Heaps and Swartz (1994) point out that the criminal justice system plays an important role in treatment through the "threat of increased sanctions for noncompliance . . . to motivate some individuals to continue in and comply with treatment protocols until they internalize the motivation to succeed at treatment" (p. 197). The United States General Accounting Office has endorsed increased use of programs such as Treatment Alternatives to Street Crime (TASC) which has proven effective in lowering recidivism and drug use among criminal justice populations through an emphasis on identifying drug-using individuals, providing assessment and ensuring appropriate treatment services (Anglin et al., 1996; U.S. General Accounting Office, 1993). Drug courts provide additional opportunities for the judicial system to utilize treatment as an alternative to incarceration, while judges act as case managers in addressing a range of physiological, psychological and behavioral drug dependency issues (Inciardi et al., 1996).

In harm reduction, treatment, rehabilitation, and education are emphasized: Drug treatment including methadone clinic expansion as well as condom and clean needle distribution services are essential. Those in the harm reduction tradition emphasize research that shows the effectiveness of drug treatment in general populations and in the criminal justice system. A wide variety of studies show that methadone maintenance and other forms of drug treatment have been effective in reducing drug use and other high-risk behaviors. Such programs may result in decreased drug use, increased employment, and stable living arrangements (Inciardi et al., 1996; McBride & VanderWaal, 1997; Nadelmann & McNeely, 1996; Rosenbaum, Washburn, Knight, Kelley, & Irwin, 1996). Those advocating a harm reduction approach are very concerned about the availability and affordability of methadone programs. For example, federal support for methadone clinics has dropped by more than a third since the mid-1980s while fees required of addicts have risen by 80% (Anglin & McGlothlin, 1985; California Department of Alcohol and Drug Programs, 1991; Gerstein & Harwood, 1990; Rosenbaum et al., 1996). Estimates place the number of needed methadone clinics at four times the number currently operating if services are to be available to all heroin addicts wanting treatment (Goode, 1997).

Because harm reduction approaches to the drug policy debate emphasize reducing all types of harm resulting from drug abuse, condom and needle distribution programs are vital components. Drug abuse is well-recognized as a primary risk factor in transmission of HIV due to injection drug use and unprotected sexual activity (Chitwood et al., 1991). Current political trends aside, HIV risk reduction programs emphasizing the safer use of needles and the use of condoms have been proved effective in lowering risk from HIV both nationally (Needle & Coyle, 1997) and internationally (McBride, Inciardi, Surratt, Terry, & Van Buren, 1998).

In a national harm reduction policy, education programs would move away from a "Just Say No" assumption of zero tolerance to one that emphasizes the amelioration of the most harmful consequences of use. According to Rosenbaum (1996, pp. 11-13), harm reduction education programs would rest on four assumptions:

- "Drugs" must be categorized to include all intoxicating substances, including those which are legal.

- Total abstinence is not realistic.

- It is possible to use drugs in a controlled, responsible way, and the use of mind-altering substances does not necessarily constitute abuse.

- Nothing is more crucial regarding safe drug use than context (pharmacology, psychological state of user, and setting/social group).

Goals of harm reduction education based on these assumptions would address factual risks and benefits of drug use, incorporate youths' experience and expertise, teach methods of safer use, and emphasize positive role models (Bertram et al., 1996; Rosenbaum, 1996).

Harm reduction proponents also argue that an "apolitical public health focus" approach to drug policy is not enough (Price, 1996). Comprehensive approaches that address the causes of drug abuse and which incorporate cultural and environmental aspects must be included in any proposed policy solutions (see Heaps & Swartz, 1994). Stronger regulations limiting the advertising industry (including alcohol and tobacco products), an inclusive national health care policy, and economic development plans would be key points in harm reduction policy. As Bertram et al. (1996) note, "A modest, intelligent policy aimed at solving immediate inner-city problems would go a long way toward promoting public health in general as well as toward preventing the problems of drug abuse. Small steps toward job creation, child care opportunities, improved schools, adequate housing, and safer streets would make a significant difference" (p. 212).

Critics of Harm Reduction

Concerns about harm reduction policy exist on both sides of the continuum. Prohibitionists further counter that harm reduction policy changes will result in a loss of hard-won gains in the war against drugs and increase the acceptance of drug use in the general population resulting in actual increased use (Martinez, 1992). Prohibitionists are also concerned that programs such as needle exchange (a) do not provide a chance for recovery from drug addiction and (b) have not been conclusively proven to reduce the spread of AIDS (Martinez, 1992). There is also some skepticism about the effectiveness of treatment. Critics of treatment note that long-term effectiveness is often minimal and that significant reductions in use tend to occur after 15 years of heavy use with or without treatment (Moran, 1994). Additional concerns focus on the definition of harm: What harm level is safe? Is the developmental harm due to a high school student's chronic use of marijuana (lack of motivation and increased likelihood to not complete an education) safe? Would the policy lead to increased numbers of addicts in order to potentially reduce crime and/or the numbers of drug-induced deaths? Others are wary about further involving the government in regulation and program services. From this perspective, harm reduction alone without decriminalization would simply continue a failed policy of ineffective governmental involvement in personal behavior and property rights (Szasz, 1996).

Medical Models

Medical models of drug policy reform are based on the premise that drug abuse and addiction are diseases that require and can be ameliorated most successfully by medical treatment methods. Groups such as Physician Leadership on National Drug Policy emphasize medically based approaches to reducing harmful illegal drug use: "Addiction to illegal drugs is a chronic illness. Addiction treatment requires continuity of care, including acute and follow-up care strategies, management of any relapses, and satisfactory outcome measurements" (Public Health Reports, 1997). Medical models state that criminal justice system- and interdiction-driven drug policy approaches cannot adequately address illegal drug use (Public Health Reports, 1997). They propose that currently illicit substances be placed under the control of physicians who would then prescribe them to individuals who claim to be dependent on a specific drug.

Outcomes and level of physician intervention vary depending upon the model; however, all emphasize the role of physicians as working with the patient in providing needed pharmacotherapeutic treatment. Three overall models of treatment are available: maintenance, adversarial, and interference approaches. Maintenance models view the use of psychoactive substances as a user's attempt to bring his/her possibly lower levels of endorphins up to functional levels. However, street-level illicit substances are often corrupted with additives or are too short-acting to effectively improve the user's endorphin levels. Programs for opioid dependence such as methadone maintenance treatment (MMT) provide methadone to improve duration of the needed high and suppression of withdrawal (Marsch, 1998), whereas levomethadyl acetate hydrochloride (LAAM) assists by lessening withdrawal symptoms as well as lowering narcotic effects (Lewis, 1998). Whereas the goal of MMT and LAAM is continued and more responsible use or maintenance, both the adversarial and interference approaches have the goal of slow withdrawal and eventual, full discontinuation of use. Antabuse is an example of a more adversarial approach to assisting alcoholics in controlling their excessive drinking, causing violent nausea when alcohol is consumed. On the other hand, Ibogaine is an example of a neurotransmitter antagonist. Ibogaine is specifically designed to interfere with an addict's desire for cocaine or morphine by blocking the release of dopamine in the neural pathways affected by the two drugs, thereby lowering cravings for either drug (Sisko, 1992).

In addition to targeting the illness of addiction through treatment and prevention, medicalization policy would involve the utilization of "procedures which are shown to be effective" in the criminal justice system in reducing supply and demand (Public Health Reports, 1997), improving access to addiction treatment programs and eliminating the social stigma associated with diagnosis and treatment of drug problems (Lewis, 1998; *Public Health Reports*, 1997).

Critics of Medical Models

The concept of treatment-on-demand is central to medical models. However, as Sisko (1995) points out, the concepts of both treatment and demand are problematic. What modality(ies) of treatment would be involved? Who would be demanding such treatment? Would it be the addicts themselves judging what would best suit their needs, or would those in authoritarian positions such as the judicial system or employers designate "appropriate treatment"? What of the individuals who would not choose to seek medical supervision and yet were chronically addicted? In addition, the current movement toward privatization and managed care emphasizes efficiency—not the time-intensive services needed for chronic addiction whereby providers must often plan for and expect relapse care. In such an environment, it is essential that treatment—for the poor and uninsured as well as for those with adequate financial resources—be greatly expanded and provided on demand.

Medical Marijuana

One of the hottest issues in the current drug policy debate falls under the auspices of medicalization: medical marijuana. In 1996, both California and Arizona passed proposals allowing the medical use of marijuana: Proposition 215 (California's Compassionate Use Act), and Proposition 200 (Arizona's Drug Medicalization, Prevention and Control Act). Specifically, the primary purpose of the California act is to

> provide a specified group of patients with an affirmative defense to the charge of possession or cultivation of marijuana, the defense of medical necessity. To use this defense, the patient must be able to show that his or her physician recommended or approved of the use of marijuana, either orally or in writing. . . . Nothing in this law changes current law against buying or selling marijuana or affects federal law; it merely provides that qualified patients and their primary care givers can possess and cultivate their own marijuana

for personal medicinal purposes, without violating state drug laws.
(Annas, 1997, p. 435)

The Arizona legislation went a step beyond California, permitting
any Schedule I drug (those with a high potential for abuse, no
currently accepted medical use and a lack of accepted safety for
use under medical supervision) to be prescribed by a physician.
However, in April 1997, Proposition 200 was effectively blocked by
an amendment limiting the coverage to those substances with FDA
approval. As of spring 1998, 23 states had laws that, in some way,
support the medicinal use of marijuana (National Organization for
the Reform of Marijuana Laws, 1998). Organizations such as the
American Bar Association and the American Medical Association, as
well as nationally reputable publications such as *New England Journal of Medicine* support the initiatives (Annas, 1997; Chon, 1997;
Stempsey, 1998).

Support for the medical use of marijuana centers on the drug's
efficacy in five main areas: appetite stimulation, controlling nausea
and vomiting, neurologic and movement disorders, analgesia, and
glaucoma (Voelker, 1997). Cancer and AIDS patients as well as those
suffering from paraplegia, multiple sclerosis, insomnia, post-traumatic
stress disorder, anorexia, anxiety, psoriasis, and drug addiction have
all been listed as finding relief through marijuana that could not be
obtained through other medical avenues (Pollan, 1997). The federal
government, however, has taken a strongly antagonistic stance toward the initiatives, threatening physicians who recommend marijuana to patients with both investigation and loss of prescription
privileges under Drug Enforcement Administration regulations
(Annas, 1997; Federal News Service, 1996).

Opponents argue several issues.[2] First, a lack of proven support
for the drug's safety and effectiveness, concern for the carcinogenic
properties of any smoked substance, and the existence of substitutes
such as Dronabinol and Marinol that contain the same chemical
compounds (THC) that lead to relief of chronic symptoms of various
maladies. Second, the acceptance of medical marijuana will send a
message to the nation's youths that use of marijuana is acceptable.
Such a message will lead to increased use not only of marijuana but
of other more dangerous substances (the "gateway" drug theory).
Third, issues of regulation on who could prescribe, level of proof to

Figure 2.1. *Doonesbury* © 1998 G. B. Trudeau. Reprinted with permission of *Universal Press Syndicate.* All rights reserved.

31

confirm need, methods of distribution and the potential for corruption have not been adequately addressed. Fourth, Americans are largely antilegalization.

Supporters counter these arguments by stating that the use of marijuana is not a cure but an essential part of the pharmacopeia in treating chronically ill patients, many of whom may not be able to continue treatments without the therapeutic benefits of the drug. Existing substitutes carry their own problems, such as difficulty in ascertaining therapeutic dosage. With regard to concerns about the implementation of such a program, the San Jose Police Department has been reasonably successful in creating a working solution to having medical marijuana as part of the social fabric: Inventory methods, purchasing quantity limits, and location of distribution have been addressed (Pollan, 1997). Also, even though the majority of Americans are against drug legalization, statistics change when the issue of medical use of substances is introduced. An ABC news poll conducted in May 1997 found 69% of Americans in support of the legalization of medical marijuana (Pollan, 1997).

Clearly, the debate caused by medical marijuana is joining the movement within the United States away from "Just Say No" to a more careful consideration of alternative drug policy positions. In the existing continuum of the drug policy debates, medical models could be viewed as an additional piece of almost any position (except that of strict punitive prohibition). Aspects of harm reduction, legalization/regulation, and partial decriminalization are all present. The main focus of the model, if accepted, is that the medical community be a key player in regulating the substance use of users whose primary motivation is maintenance, not recreation (Goode, 1997).

Legalization/Regulation

Those taking a drug legalization position generally strongly agree with the criticisms of current prohibition policy. They believe that prohibition has failed to reduce drug use and has eroded civil rights, overwhelmed the criminal justice system, and caused considerable public health consequences, including the high rate of AIDS among some types of drug users. In addition, there is a tendency to believe that the behavior and psychopharmacological consequences of drug use have been overstated by the "drug warriors." However, perhaps through the recognition that an unregulated free market of powerful psychoactive drugs would have severe societal consequences, those advocating some form of legalization do not appear to want legalized drugs to be manufactured and marketed by unregulated private corporations. They usually suggest that some type of licensing or regulatory approach be used with currently illegal drugs and are often in harmony with harm reduction and medicalization.

The legalization/regulation solution recognizes the reality of drug use—the demand factor—and attempts to minimize social and individual harm by providing drugs through the safest and most inexpensive means possible. There is a belief among legalizers that a basic rate of drug use exists in all human populations that is little affected by law enforcement. Those advocating legalization argue that severity and certainty of punishment have only minor deterrence effects on human behavior (for a discussion of the limited effect of deterrence, see Barkan, 1997). There is also a strong belief that a factual, nonexaggerated approach to drug education combined with consumer observation would result in a relatively low rate of drug consumption. Admittedly, there might be an initial increase in drug use after legalization, but the expectation seems to be that the vast majority of rational consumers would not use legalized drugs if provided with the facts. Some type of governmental regulation or licensing would be required to specify who could obtain drugs (in terms of prior use and/or age).

Those advocating this position are also concerned about drug use among youths. Regulations and licensing would be implemented to attempt to restrict use by minors. Supporters often draw analogies to current regulations on alcohol and tobacco (for a discussion of alcohol control implications for drug policy reform, see Levine & Reinarman, 1993). Supporters acknowledge that alcohol and tobacco are not well-regulated; at present, youths use these substances at high rates and report having no difficulty obtaining them. Implementation of this perspective might result in increased regulation of tobacco and alcohol.

The result of a legalization approach would be to focus on appropriate distribution of drugs. Penalties would target distributors who ignored regulations, not users. For legalizers, it is important that there be no significant profit motive for the distribution of legalized drugs. It is believed that the profit motive is integrally involved in the failure of alcohol and tobacco regulations to prevent distribution of these substances to youths. As Kurt Schmoke has said, "Under this [legalization/regulation] alternative to the War on Drugs, the government would set up a regulatory regime to pull addicts into the public health system. The government, not criminal traffickers, would control the price, distribution, and purity of addictive substances" (cited in Buckley & Nadelmann, 1996; for further discussion of legalization positions, see Gazzaniga, 1995; Goode, 1997; Nadelmann, 1989).

Those advocating legalizing drugs often point to (a) the apparent successes of the Dutch legalization of marijuana and considerable tolerance of other forms of drug use and (b) the more recent Swiss legalization experiment in Zurich. Legalizers argue that their approach would have a number of very specific advantages:

- Removal of profit (and therefore capitalization) from criminal organizations

- Considerable reduction in criminal activity of all types both directly and indirectly related to drug use

- Alleviation of overcrowded court dockets and prisons

- Focus of the criminal justice system on serious crimes rather than on private personal behavior

- Significant reductions in the health consequences of use, including overdosage due to unknown purity and reactions to contaminants as well as consequences associated with contaminated implements of ingestion that result in hepatitis, HIV infection, and other serious health consequences

- Cessation of civil rights erosion

Critics of Legalization/Regulation

The legalization/regulation policy alternatives rest on a basic assumption that government can effectively regulate the use of the legalized substances. It is curious that those who are so profoundly critical of the government's ability to prohibit are enthusiastic about its ability to regulate. Although those who advocate a legalization position are often disdainful of those who ask for specifics, the fact remains that legalization advocates have effectively argued the weaknesses in current policy but have not sufficiently addressed weaknesses in their own. These include the following:

- Age of legalization for specific substances and the rationale for those ages

- Mechanisms of distribution or licensing and how the profit motive would be addressed. Licensed distribution implies private corporations; what restrictions would be placed on their interest in increasing distribution through some form of advertising? How would the government address issues surrounding the distribution of powerful addictive substances to disadvantaged minority groups?

- Issues of potency, intoxication levels, and distribution liability

- The utter failure of current regulation policies for tobacco and alcohol to prevent the use of these substances by youths

- Penalties for failure to comply with the regulatory requirements. Would such penalties involve loss of the right to distribute, or would they involve criminal penalties for continued violations?

It is certainly possible that these issues could be successfully addressed; however, such clarifications need to happen before legalization can have a chance for a serious hearing at the national level. Legalization approaches do raise very important criticisms of current policy and do provide serious alternatives, but they often fail to recognize the complexity of this era's increasing distaste for governmental regulation. Those who advocate decriminalization particularly focus their criticisms on what they regard as the paternalistic elements of regulation. Szasz (1996) argues that legalization would be just another failed paternalistic attempt to involve the government in private behavior and the control of private property. He sees both prohibition and legalization as part of the failed, liberty-destructive 20th-century socialistic experiment.

Decriminalization

The decriminalization position emerged most clearly during the past decade. Supporters forcefully argued that current national drug policy has failed to prevent recent increases in youth drug use while succeeding in eroding basic civil rights, overwhelming the criminal justice system, and eroding public support for law enforcement. Many of those who today advocate for decriminalization previously supported medicalization or some type of mild regulation. However, they have become much more radical: They believe that almost any type of government prohibition or regulation is doomed to failure and will bring about enormously negative civil and moral consequences. As Arnold Trebach has said, "I have come to believe that the urban situation in America is so desperate as to demand the nearly immediate dismantling of drug prohibition" (in Trebach & Inciardi, 1993, p. 13).

Decriminalization has many similarities to other "reform" positions: It consistently calls for more humane treatment of drug addicts, including physician treatment. The position also seems to advocate elements of harm reduction: Supporters want accurate, scientifically based information about drugs and their real effects available to the public. Most also urge distribution of paraphernalia as the avenue of the safest possible use. Decriminalization also resembles the legalization/regulation perspective in that supporters wish to immediately remove criminal penalties from drug use. However, one crucial difference divides the two positions. That difference rests on John Stuart Mill's philosophy as presented in his book *On Liberty* (1921). Mill concluded that the government has no business prohibiting or even regulating the personal choice of free citizens (for further presentation of the decriminalization perspective, see Trebach in Trebach & Inciardi, 1993, as well as the bimonthly journal *Drug Policy Letter*).

Unlike other perspectives along the drug policy continuum, the decriminalization approach does not attempt to develop complex alternatives that involve using government-mandated harm reduction, public health education, prevention, or intervention. It does not necessarily advocate utilizing the medical community to manage addiction. It certainly does not want the increased complexity of governmental regulation. The decriminalization perspective seems to imply that all other alternatives have many of the same inherent weaknesses that bedevil current prohibition policy: namely, that any attempt by government to regulate drugs has an inherent potential for abuse.

The decriminalization perspective simply wants to eliminate laws that prohibit or regulate the manufacture or distribution of current illegal drugs. While there are partial and full decriminalizers, the basic position is that of libertarianism. As such, government should not be involved in either prohibition or regulation of the private behavioral or property choices of its citizens—even if such policies may be deemed to be in the interest of the citizens. Perhaps this is most clearly stated by Thomas Szasz (Friedman & Szasz, 1992): "I favor free trade in drugs . . . in a free society it is none of the government's business what ideas a man puts into his mind; likewise, it should be none of its business what drugs he puts into his body." Friedman and Szasz (1992) essentially argue for a return to the consumerism policy of the 19th century with use levels determined by intelligent, educated consumers.

Another leading proponent of decriminalization, Arnold Trebach, also argues for giving back to people a right taken away from them by government early in this century—the right to freely choose to use drugs: "My preferred plan of legalization [decriminalization] seeks essentially to turn the clock back to the last century" (Trebach & Inciardi, 1993, p. 79). In a book entitled *Our Right to Drugs*, Szasz (1996) argues that drugs are a form of property and, as such, the government has no right to interfere with how free citizens use their private property.

This position has some attractive strengths. It is rooted in the basic assumptions of a free and democratic society. These include the assumption that citizens are self-governing and capable of exercising self-control and good citizenship without the paternalistic intrusiveness of government as overseer. Within this tradition, there is also the belief that a free society must accept as the price of freedom that a proportion of its citizens will make decisions that may be harmful to the health, happiness or longevity of those citizens. This position seems to be, to an extent, in touch with the political trends of the era. There is currently little interest in a large intrusive government; indeed, there has been a devolution of authority from national government to local government to individual responsibility. Distrust of government is very high. Adoption of decriminalization-based policy would involve minimal government intrusion or regulation. This perspective further points toward the enormous amounts of money that would be saved as inappropriate governmental intrusion into private citizen choices is eliminated. A decriminalization policy would allow the police to focus on behavior that clearly harms other citizens while preventing the justice system from interfering with individual behavior that harms no one but the user (see Stares, 1996a, 1996b).

Criticisms of Decriminalization

Each of the other drug policy positions has implicit or explicit criticisms of decriminalization (see Inciardi in Trebach & Inciardi, 1993, for a comprehensive critique of decriminalization). Basic criticisms of decriminalization focus on a significant underestimation of the social and economic harm of increased drug use, a misunderstanding of the nature of addiction and initiation processes and a naive confidence in the free market. Critics of decriminalization argue that harm resulting from drug abuse is not individual but systemic. It thereby fulfills the criteria elucidated by Mill (1921) to warrant societal concern. Harms arising from drug abuse include psychopharmacological effects related to violence as well as significant health care costs. Substance use plays a significant role in accidents that also injure nonusers. In addition, the nostalgic view of 19th-century America may not be reflected in the reality of those who experienced that century. It was a century without access to health care and without any type of welfare safety net. There was minimal recognition of governmental or societal responsibility for those who needed health or human services. Although government is reducing its sense of responsibility for many of these services, there still seems to be an expectation of some responsibility for its citizens. We are no longer in a society of isolated nonintegrated parts. It may be difficult to separate what is only harmful to the individual from what is also costly to society. If there is an expectation of societal aid, then there may be an expectation of societal regulations. Indeed, Szasz (1996) argues that as long as society makes others pay for the health care costs of drug users society will have the incentive to regulate drug use. Szasz appears to advocate dismantling publicly funded health care and placing the responsibility of payment on those who make the choice to use drugs (Szasz in Buckley & Nadelmann, 1996).

It also seems that the decriminalization position may not recognize the complexity or implications of addictive substances in a free market treatment. The very nature of addiction limits free choice. One can perhaps construct a notion that free choice occurs the first few times an individual uses an addictive substance, but that choice disappears as addiction becomes an experienced reality. This position further fails to recognize the role that advertising can be allowed to play in a free market economy. The logical culmination of a true policy of decriminalization whereby there is only minimal if any governmental regulation or penalties would be an equally free environment for advertising drugs. In turn, this onslaught of publicity would have serious ramifications on youth populations. Serious questions should be raised about the ability of youths, some as young as 13, to have the information, critical capacity, and wisdom to make a free choice about a substance that is highly addictive. A truly unregulated free market would have few if any barriers to prevent drug use by youths. It is self-evident that decriminalizers do not advocate drug use by youths nor see youths as necessarily having the capacity to make informed decisions about drug use. Rather, decriminalizers focus on drug use as an adult choice. However, as noted by Califano (1997), initiation of drug use usually occurs prior to age 21. The data simply do not support the assumption that drug use is an adult choice. Increasingly, it is the choice of youths aged 12 to 17 both for initiation and continuing use. Recently released data from the National Household Survey show that about 11% of youths aged 12 to 17 used an illegal drug in the past month. About 30% reported use in the past year. Further, youths aged 12 to 17 were more likely to use an illegal drug in the past month than individuals aged 26 and over (CESAR, 1998). These data indicate that it is not adults who are choosing to use drugs; rather, it is the very population that decriminalizers say they specifically do not wish to see using drugs—America's youths. Decriminalization policies would seem to be particularly weak in preventing youth drug use.

A focus on decriminalization for a national drug policy also raises serious questions about our current national expectations of a free market. Our society and the world in general seem to be enamored with the concept. The free market is seen as providing the best chance for economic strength, political freedom, civil rights, and, it appears, even human happiness. This era seems to have extraordinary faith in the free market to solve everything, even drug abuse. The free market may be the best producer of high-quality, cost-effective products and services, but it may not be the best policy for dealing with addictive substances. Issues of marketing, target marketing, and the human cost of increased drug abuse seem to be naively ignored by advocates of decriminalization. The effective critical capacity that is applied by decriminalizers to the current prohibition position seems strangely absent in the examination of their own assumptions and the very real consequences that might result from the adoption of this position.

■ A Market-Driven Reality?

Positions in the drug policy discussion provide an interesting jumble of views on the role of the economy and any reforms that may be needed. Some positions do not address the role of the economy at all; others believe massive reforms are needed, and still others (like the decriminalization perspective) believe that a hands-off free market approach offers the only hope for ameliorating the current frustrations, dangers, and unknowns of substance use.

Prohibition has two main camps on the issue. Strict prohibitionists concentrate on punitive measures to suppress illegal activity and address the economy only through the threat of incarceration to prevent involvement in the lucrative drug market—either using or selling and distributing. Moderate prohibitionists, with their public health views, combine a punitive approach with concern about the role of the economy in creating or limiting opportunities for jobs and educational advancement and the influence of such opportunities on substance use. Harm reduction advocates are often the most vocal about the need for economic reforms—including jobs and educational opportunities—calling for a systems-level approach addressing all aspects of substance use. Medical models do not usually directly address the role of economics in substance use, focusing instead on the maintenance and health-related aspects of the discussion. Legalization/regulation acknowledges the role of economic forces through its concern over the existing black markets and their incentives to engage in the drug trade caused by prohibition. Such policies suggest governmental removal of economic incentives by regulation of illicit substances in the same way that alcohol and tobacco are currently controlled. Finally, decriminalization firmly believes that the economy holds the key to the dilemma caused by psychoactive substances: Rational choice and the free market system are the only answers to the policy discussion.

How important are economic considerations to the drug policy debate? Essential, according to Hagedorn (1997, 1998). Hagedorn conducted a 5-year study on the drug economy in two middle- to high-range drug-dealing neighborhoods in Milwaukee, Wisconsin. Economic restructuring has meant an overall movement of lucrative jobs out of the cities and into the suburbs throughout the nation, leaving the poor to struggle with decisions over how to survive. Existing jobs based on information technology require education and training often unavailable to workers in poor communities. Hagedorn (1998) notes that there is a fundamentally "lower class response by men and women with little formal education and few formal skills" (p. 3) to form their own business opportunities when existing jobs are beyond their abilities or simply not available. Although some of these businesses are legal, many enterprises in poor neighborhoods are "off the books" and include streetside car repair operations, haircutting and unreported child care in private homes, street vending, sales of questionable goods, ad hoc house painting companies, and drug selling. "Being poor and not finishing high school does not mean a person is lazy or dumb and doomed to go nowhere. If the jobs won't be created by either the public or the private sector, then poor people will have to create the jobs themselves. And they are doing just that" (Hagedorn, 1998, p. 3). Such entrepreneurial spirit is a core part of American culture, as is the desire of most gang members in the study (male and female) to obtain a decent job and raise a family (Hagedorn, 1997).

Many of those Hagedorn studied combined licit with drug-selling income sources in order to be financially stable: "Over the years 1989-1991, gang members interviewed made an average of $2400 per month selling drugs and less than $700 per month in licit jobs. Still, most worked more months in the low wage jobs than selling drugs" (Hagedorn, 1997, p. 1). White male gang members were more likely to find full-time jobs by their mid-20s than African American and Latino males: more than two thirds to one fourth, respectively (Hagedorn, 1997). At least 10% of all male Latinos and African Americans in the two neighborhoods studied were supported, in some way, by the drug business. Hagedorn notes that almost all female gang members in the study left the gangs by age 20, and no notice-able increase of women in the drug economy was seen. However, Hagedorn also notes that welfare reform may well have an increasingly negative impact on women as it may ultimately force them to seek financial sources in illicit areas.

Hagedorn (1998) believes the large racial discrepancies within the criminal justice population incarcerated for drug use represent not simply a rampantly discriminatory criminal justice system but one that reflects the trends of the informal economy: "Those being arrested for drug offenses are mainly minority males who are being supported by the drug business. Whites, who use most of the cocaine, but who are not as involved with drugs as an economic industry, are simply not arrested nor prosecuted to nearly the same extent" (p. 3). Interestingly, drug selling as a business was most lucrative—and most organized—when gangs sold to Whites and/or noncommunity members (Hagedorn, 1997). Hagedorn found that in poor, minority communities the drug business fulfills important economic and entrepreneurial needs, whereas it remains a social role in predominantly White suburbs where economic opportunities are more available (for further discussion of the involvement of limited role opportunities in the decision to become a street drug dealer, see Stephens, 1991).

Hagedorn's study is obviously not nationwide, but it brings up two very important issues: Economic restructuring has caused a severe shortage of viable jobs for the minority poor, and entrepreneurial businesses are playing a large role in providing stable resources for minority populations, with drug selling just one type of these businesses. Hagedorn (1998) points out that current prohibition policy does not create jobs for the minority poor and results in high incarceration costs. However, he cautions against simple jobs programs. Such programs often provide low-paying and low-skilled positions which may not provide enough incentive to discontinue drug businesses. His recommendations include the following:

- Distinctions made in legal repercussions between nonviolent economic activity and violent crime/use of firearms, including elimination of criminal penalties for the possession or sale of small amounts of illicit substances

- Alternatives to incarceration expanded, such as drug treatment and job training

- Values and conflict mediation programs available in schools and social programs

- Increased investment in central-city neighborhoods

- Encouragement of tax credits and subsidies for new, licit businesses

- Links between the private sector and entrepreneurial training

- Expanded child care and job training for poor mothers

- To the extent possible, elimination of handgun possession

- Increased emphasis on collaboration between gang members/drug users and the research community in research efforts

Hagedorn's work calls all positions in the drug policy debate to reevaluate the importance of economics. Policy positions must address the fact that, at present, the market-driven reality of the drug business involves not only the powerful motivating factors of addiction (which, in actuality, renders the concept of "rational choice" untenable), but also the need for an informal economy to support the nation's minority poor. The bottom line is this: Can the drug policy discussion continuum afford to ignore the need for economic reform? The answer is no.

■ Discussion

It was about a decade ago that two of the authors (Inciardi & McBride, 1989) of this chapter first examined national drug policy, its critiques, and possible alternatives. In the past 10 years, much has changed. Youth smoking rates are climbing rapidly for both tobacco and marijuana, perceptions of risk and disapproval for marijuana have declined among high school populations, and state initiatives have adopted nonprohibition approaches to medical marijuana use. Although there have been minimal changes in the past 5 years, the majority of arrestees in the United States are still current illegal drug users, often of cocaine. Most of the individuals arrested who test positive for drug use are members of minority groups (Arrestee Drug Abuse Monitoring Program, 1998). Yet general societal surveys indicate that Whites have the highest use rates. There have been significant changes in the proportion of juvenile arrestees who test positive for an illegal drug. In most of the cities involved in testing juvenile arrestees for the presence of an illegal drug, the proportion of juveniles that have tested positive has doubled since early 1993. For example, in Cleveland, Ohio, about 30% of juvenile arrestees tested positive for an illegal drug in the first quarter of 1993. By the last quarter of 1997, this had risen to over 60%. It certainly appears that the punitive approach has not been a deterrent (Arrestee Drug Abuse Monitoring Program, 1998).

Current drug policy has simply not been effective in reducing the rates of illegal drug use in the past decade or preventing their increase in the general or juvenile justice populations. In addition, the regulatory approach to tobacco seems to have done nothing to prevent a dramatic increase among youths smoking. In addition, the corruption effect of both punitive and regulatory policies seems to be significant. Prohibition has continued to raise serious questions about its effect on civil rights, differential focus on minorities, and increasingly come to be seen as blind to its own consequences. There is clearly a need to rethink national substance use policy. The past 10 years have seen the further development of a wide variety of alternative drug policy positions: continued prohibition, harm reduction, medicalization, legalization/regulation, and decriminalization. Amidst all of these policy movements, it is important to note that the majority of Americans do not want to legalize or decriminalize drugs, not even marijuana. There still appears to be a strong political consensus that current illegal drugs are illegal for a reason; they are harmful and should not be legalized or decriminalized and allowed to enter into the free market. However, a free society simply cannot arrest and incarcerate a significant portion of its population (although our society appears to be testing this very limit). A "Just Say No" campaign with no regard to underlying psychological, social, or economic reasons for use is simply naive and ineffective. It is important to consider other drug policies.

The medicalization movement has gained some support in the past decade. It appears that society believes that whatever pharmaceuticals are necessary to relieve human suffering should be made available. There appears to be significant interest in combining regulation and medicalization, thereby providing physicians with the right to prescribe such substances as deemed necessary. The view appears to be that drug policy, in its attempt to prevent the use of illegal drugs, has very little place in a physician-patient relationship, an important stance as methadone maintenance remains a significant part of the drug treatment system. Medical interventionist look toward science and its developments in different types of neurotransmitter agonists or antagonists to treat addiction. Meanwhile, other elements of medicalization appear to receive less support. There appears to be little interest either from society or from the medical establishment for allowing physicians to distribute current illegal drugs in a legalization/regulation policy.

To date, legalization/regulation has not worked well. It has utterly failed to be effective in preventing the increase in tobacco use among youths or lowering alcohol use rates. The movement still suffers from a lack of detail. Issues such as age of legal use and the control of distribution are not well elucidated. As decriminalizers noted, regulation enforcement discussions seem to move very close to a prohibition criminalization stand. Perhaps most important, this does not seem to be an era for the creation of another massive federal or state bureaucracy to regulate behavior or society.

Decriminalization, except for small amounts of marijuana, does not appear to be attracting significant social support. Although this position calls for a return to a 19th-century drug policy position, we do not live in the 19th century. That century had no health insurance or assumption of societal obligation toward the sick or dysfunctional. Admittedly, we are reducing this assumption today. Perhaps the decriminalization movement is consistent with the trend to disengage national responsibility for those who need health and human services. However, assuming there is still some expectation of that function, it is difficult to accept that society can afford the free market advertising and distribution of substances that cause significant behavioral, economic, and health consequences. We are no longer (and certainly have not been for a long time) in a society of self-sufficient, nonintegrated parts. Society does not appear to believe that it is better off with an old drug policy model that would very likely significantly increase substance use and all of its consequences. Although the free marketing of highly addictive products may be a capitalist's fantasy come true, it does not appear to be a part of the vision of general society.

If these policies have significant problems, where does that leave the national debate? It leaves a type of harm reduction policy coupled with an increased focus on economic development and opportunities. This combination might offer some realistic and politically acceptable opportunities for policy reform. Acceptable and effective harm reduction policies might include (a) the increased use of drug treatment instead of incarceration, (b) increased utilization of effective educational and prevention programs for youths based on the best scientific data and presented via an effective medium, and (c) efforts to ameliorate the consequences of substance use, including needle exchange, the use of bleach, or any method of use that reduces the health consequences of addictive psychoactive substances.

The seemingly boundless enthusiasm for incarceration in our society has often blinded us to alternatives for drug users. The research literature strongly indicates that a significant portion of criminal behavior is drug driven. Thus, it is fairly logical to use an approach that can address underlying causes of criminal behavior—drug treatment. Critics of treatment often point out that although there may be positive changes in comparison to some sort of control group the changes are often relatively small and the rate of drug use remains fairly high during and after treatment. Data suggest that this criticism has merit. However, incarceration is much worse: It simply has no impact on subsequent drug use. There is no improvement, and incarceration is very costly. As TASC and other evaluations have shown, treatment has a positive effect in criminal justice populations and does not jeopardize public safety.

Harm reduction positions make an important point when they emphasize the necessity of a proactive education approach. This approach must be based on careful research into the best methods to communicate to youths. It must be based on accurate—not demonized—information and must be presented by credible sources. Also, education and prevention messages must have sufficient funding if they are to have any hope of competing with the almost unlimited resources of tobacco advertisers and the positive imaging of other drugs in the mass media. The same level of effective creativity must be applied to drug education and prevention that is applied to the creation of market demand. The harm reduction perspective would also imply the necessity of teaching safer practices for those already using. Data clearly show that needle exchange and bleach can prevent the transmission of HIV and a host of other infectious diseases. This basic public health approach is essential. Considerable work needs to be done not only at the national level but also at the local level to build community support for risk reduction and not just total prevention.

Finally, it is important to recognize that law and law enforcement have an appropriate role to play in national and local substance use policy. As noted many times in this chapter, there is considerable support in this nation and around the world to keep the production, distribution and use of a variety of drugs such as heroin and cocaine illegal. There is an emerging view that law enforcement must focus on major distribution points and less on street dealers. In addition, it should provide treatment opportunities as a part of incarceration, pretrial or diversion programming and probation. Data consistently show that treatment within a law enforcement and judicial environment can be successful.

Theory and Economic Reality

Perhaps even more important than treatment, education, or an appropriate use of law enforcement itself is to have a national drug policy that is driven by strong, empirically based theoretical understandings of the etiology of drug use. Such a theoretically based policy can take disparate findings and provide an integrating framework. The theory used must be applicable to today's political and cultural milieu, not to that of a few decades ago. World society has moved to an international economy with a free flow of ideas, capital, and the production of products and services. This has meant that opportunity structures are fluid and can move rapidly. The ensuing globalization of society and economy has resulted in considerable disruption of local opportunities. Just as our world has experienced this fluid globalization shift, the United States' federal government has emphasized a devolution of authority and responsibility to local communities (often without accompanying resources). The disruption of opportunity structures caused by global economic and social structural changes (including mass migration movements) must now be dealt with locally, often without the resources or context of national policy.

The need to address concepts of change and conflict arising from such social upheaval requires an understanding of human thought and interaction. Urban sociology—specifically agency-structure integration—provides a foundation from which to understand state and public policy, socioeconomic-level power structures, citizen coalitions, and global market forces, all operating to form distinct local systems (Flanagan, 1993). Three aspects of this theoretical perspective are pertinent to the drug policy discussion.

- Social action at the local level is key to determining social structure; "attention should be turned from global theories of the world system, dependency, and restructuring, toward the local level where the powerful and the less powerful face choices about how to live today and plan for tomorrow. These are the agents, great and small, who, through their individual and collective choices, are reconstituting society" (Flanagan, 1993, p. 141; see also Giddens, 1984, 1989).

- Culture is an integral component in human interaction affecting both societal structural issues and individual-group relations (Ritzer, 1996; see also Archer, 1988).

- Any level of urban analysis must acknowledge three forces shaping human interaction: (1) the overall structure operating on a Marxist economic base, (2) a managerial structure using both an economic and a political power base, and (3) an individual behavioral structure based on experience/subjectivity (Flanagan, 1993; see also Cadwallader, 1988).

Drug policy must acknowledge forces of local-level social action, culture, and economic and political power structures. As Hagedorn's research has shown, street drug dealing is a viable, available economic opportunity for many urban youths. Drug use and drug dealing—with all of their consequences—must be seen in their etiological entirety. Any attempt at providing only treatment without addressing the macro- to microsocioeconomic contexts that produced use and dealing will be of limited value. Psychological or even biomedical interventions without the etiological social context will be ineffective. A wide variety of research has shown that a collaborative multisystems approach to intervention is crucial to effectiveness (Henggeler, Pickrel, & Brondino, 1997; McBride et al., 1997). This means a recognition and elaboration of all social, economic, familial, and other systems that play a part in addressing substance abuse in an individual's life. It also means recognizing that substance use takes place within the context of macroeconomics and social structure. As Hagedorn states, "We can't solve the drug problem without recognizing its economic dimensions" (quoted in Cole, 1998, p. 18).

▮ Notes

1. The positions used here have been taken from Goode (1997) as the most recent extensive examination of the debate. However, readers should be aware that terminology has undergone significant changes over the past 10 years. For example, in Trebach's (1987) original publication, he uses the term "legalization" to refer to what this chapter calls "decriminalization."

2. For further discussion of these issues, see Stempsey (1998), Voclker (1997), Pollan (1997), and Goodman (1997).

▮ References

Anglin, D. M., Longshore, D., Turner, S., McBride, D. C., Inciardi, J. A., & Prendergast, M. (1996). *Studies of the functioning and effectiveness of Treatment Alternatives to Street Crime (TASC) programs: Final report.* Los Angeles: UCLA Drug Abuse Research Center.

Anglin, M. D., & McGlothlin, W. H. (1985). Methadone maintenance in California: A decade's experience. In L. Brill & C. Winick (Eds.), *The yearbook of substance use and abuse* (Vol. 3, pp. 219-280). New York: Human Sciences Press.

Annas, G. J. (1997). Reefer madness: The federal response to California's medical-marijuana law. *New England Journal of Medicine, 337*(6), 435-439.

Archer, M. S. (1988). *Culture and agency: The place of culture in social theory.* Cambridge, UK: Cambridge University Press.

Arrestee Drug Abuse Monitoring Program. (1998). *1997 annual report on adult and juvenile arrestees.* Washington, DC: National Institute of Justice Research Report.

Barkan, S. (1997). *Criminology.* Upper Saddle River, NJ: Prentice Hall.

Beers, D. (1991, July/August). Just say whoa! *Mother Jones,* pp. 36-43, 52-56.

Bennett, W. (1994, April 8). Losing the drug war without a fight. *Wall Street Journal,* p. 22.

Bertram, E., Blachman, M., Sharpe, K., & Andreas, P. (1996). *Drug war politics: The price of denial.* Berkeley: University of California Press.

Buckley, W. F., Jr., & Nadelmann, E. A. (1996). The war on drugs is lost. *National Review, 48*(2), 34-48.

Cadwallader, M. (1988). Urban geography and social theory. *Urban Geography, 9,* 227-251.

Califano, J. A. (1997). Addiction isn't freedom. *USA Today, 125,* 46-47.

California Department of Alcohol and Drug Programs. (1991, September). *Fact sheet: Methadone program licensing in California.* Sacramento: Author.

CESAR. (1998). *Preliminary results from the 1997 National Household Survey on Drug Abuse: Illicit drug use continues to rise among youth, stable among other age groups.* Adapted by CESAR from data of the Substance Abuse and Mental Health Services Administration (SAMHSA), http://www.samhsa.gov/oas/nhsda/nhsda97/httoc.htm accessed 8/21/98.

Chitwood, D. D., Inciardi, J. A., McBride, D. C., McCoy, C. B., McCoy, H. V., & Trapido, E. (1991). *A community approach to AIDS intervention.* New York: Greenwood.

Chon, G. (1997). Medical marijuana: A dream up in smoke? *Human Rights: Journal of the Section of Individual Rights & Responsibilities, 24*(4), 16-17.

Cohen, L. E., & Land, K. C. (1987). Age structure and crime: Symmetry versus asymmetry and the projection of crime rates through the 1990s. *American Sociological Review, 52,* 170-183.

Cole, W. (1998, July 13). Shhh! We don't discuss the drug biz here. *Time,* p. 18.

DuPont, R. L. (1979). Marihuana: A review of the issues regarding decriminalization and legalization. In G. M. Beschner & A. S. Friedman (Eds.), *Youth drug abuse: Problems, issues, and treatment* (pp. 279-284). Lexington, MA: Lexington Books.

Duke, S. B., & Gross, A. C. (1994, February). Casualties of war: Drug prohibition has shot gaping holes in the Bill of Rights. *Reason,* pp. 21-27.

Falco, M. (1989). *Winning the drug war: A national strategy.* New York: Priority Press Publications.

Federal News Service. (1996, December 30). *White House briefing news conference.*

Flanagan, W. G. (1993). *Contemporary urban sociology.* New York: Cambridge University Press.

Fratello, D. H. (1994). What killed Rev. Williams? And is it time to declare peace? *The Drug Policy Letter, 23,* 3-4.

Friedman, M., & Szasz, T. (1992). *On liberty and drugs.* Washington, DC: Drug Policy Foundation.

Gazzaniga, M. S. (1995, July 10). Legalizing drugs: Just say yes—an interview with Michael S. Gazzaniga. *National Review,* pp. 44-51.

Gerstein, D. R., & Harwood, H. J. (1990). *Treating drug problems* (Vol. 1). Washington, DC: National Academy Press.

Giddens, A. (1984). *The constitution of society: Outline of the theory of structuration.* Berkeley: University of California Press.

Giddens, A. (1989). A reply to my critics. In D. Held & J. G. Thompson (Eds.), *Social theory of modern societies: Anthony Giddens and his critics* (pp. 249-301). Cambridge, UK: Cambridge University Press.

Goode, E. (1997). *Between politics and reason: The drug legalization debate.* New York: St. Martin's.

Goodman, E. (1997, February 2). Clean thinking in the medical marijuana debate. *Boston Globe,* p. C7.

Hagedorn, J. (1997, October 9). *Final report of the drug posse and homegirl studies.* http://www.uwm.edu/Dept/CUIR/MajorRes/final.html accessed 7/14/98.

Hagedorn, J. (1998). The business of drug dealing in Milwaukee. *Wisconsin Policy Research Institute Report, 11*(5).

Heaps, M. M., & Swartz, J. A. (1994). *Toward a rational drug policy.* Chicago: University of Chicago Legal Forum.

Henggeler, S. W., Pickrel, S. G., & Brondino, M. J. (1997). *Multisystemic treatment of substance abusing and dependent delinquents: Outcomes for drug use, criminality, and out-of-home placement at posttreatment and 6-month follow-up.* Submitted for publication.

Inciardi, J. A. (1986). *The war on drugs: Heroin, cocaine, crime, and public policy.* Palo Alto, CA: Mayfield.

Inciardi, J. A. (1992). *The war on drugs II: Heroin, cocaine, crime, and public policy.* Mountain View, CA: Mayfield.

Inciardi, J. A., & Harrison, L. D. (in press). The concept of harm reduction. In J. A. Inciardi & L. D. Harrison (Eds.), *Harm reduction and drug control.* Thousand Oaks, CA: Sage.

Inciardi, J. A., & McBride, D. C. (1989). Legalization: A high risk alternative in the war on drugs. *American Behavioral Scientist, 32*(3), 259-289.

Inciardi, J. A., & McBride, D. C. (1990). Debating the legalization of drugs. In J. A. Inciardi (Ed.), *Handbook of drug control in the United States* (pp. 283-299). New York: Greenwood.

Inciardi, J. A., & McBride, D. C. (1991). *Treatment alternatives to street crime* (National Institute on Drug Abuse, DHHS Pub. No. 91-1749). Washington, DC: Government Printing Office.

Inciardi, J. A., McBride, D. C., & Surratt, H. L. (1998). The heroin street addict: Profiling a national population. In J. A. Inciardi & L. D. Harrison (Eds.), *Heroin in the age of crack-cocaine* (pp. 31-50). Thousand Oaks, CA: Sage.

Inciardi, J. A., McBride, D. C., & Rivers, J. E. (1996). *Drug control and the courts.* Thousand Oaks, CA: Sage.

Johnston, L. D., O'Malley, P. M., & Bachman, J. G. (1997, December 18). *Drug use among American teens shows some signs of leveling after a long rise* (News release). Ann Arbor: University of Michigan.

Johnston, L. D., O'Malley, P. M., & Bachman, J. G. (1998). *National survey results on drug use from the Monitoring the Future study, 1975-1997.* Rockville, MD: National Institutes of Health.

Kleiman, M. A. R. (1992). Neither prohibition nor legalization: Grudging toleration in drug control policy. *Daedalus, 121*(3), 53-84.

Kolb, L., & Du Mez, A. G. (1924, May 23). The prevalence and trend of drug addiction in the United States and factors influencing it. *Public Health Reports.*

Kraar, L. (1988, June). The drug trade. *Fortune,* pp. 27-38.

Lazare, D. (1990, January). The drug war is killing us. *The Village Voice,* pp. 22-29.

Levine, H. G., & Reinarman, C. (1993). From prohibition to regulation: Lessons from alcohol policy for drug policy in confronting drug policy. In R. Bayer & G. M. Oppenheimer (Eds.), *Illicit drugs in a free society* (pp. 160-193). New York: Cambridge University Press.

Lewis, D. (1998). Treatment works—the truth please. *DATA: The Brown University Digest of Addiction Theory & Application, 17*(4), 8-9.

Lindesmith, A. R. (1938). A sociological theory of addiction. *American Journal of Sociology, 43*, 593-613.

Lindesmith, A. R. (1940). "Dope fiend" mythology. *Journal of Criminal Law and Criminology, 31*, 199-208.

MacCoun, R. J., Kahan, J. P., Gillespie, J., & Rhee, J. (1993). A content analysis of the drug legalization debate. *Journal of Drug Issues, 23*(4), 615-629.

Marsch, L. A. (1998). The efficacy of methadone maintenance interventions in reducing illicit opiate use, HIV risk behavior, and criminality: A meta-analysis. *Addiction, 93*(4) 515-532.

Martinez, B. (1992). *Needle exchange programs: Are they effective?* (ONDCP Bulletin No. 7). Washington, DC: Office of National Drug Control Policy.

McBride, D. C. (1977). The relationship between drug use patterns and arrest charge. In *Drug use and crime* (pp. 409-418). Springfield, NJ: National Technical Information Service.

McBride, D. C. (1990). Generational differences in HIV risk and AIDS. *American Behavioral Scientist, 33*, 491-502.

McBride, D. C. (1995). Prohibition of drugs: Pro and con. In J. H. Jaffe (Ed.), *Encyclopedia of drugs and alcohol* (Vol. 2, pp. 826-832). New York: Simon & Schuster.

McBride, D. C., Burgman-Habermehl, C., Alpert, G., & Chitwood, D. (1986). Drugs and homicide. *Bulletin of the New York Academy of Medicine, 62*, 497-508.

McBride, D. C., & Dalton, S. G. (1977). Criminal justice diversion for whom? In A. Cohn (Ed.), *Criminal justice planning and development* (pp. 103-116). Beverly Hills, CA: Sage.

McBride, D. C., Inciardi, J. A., Surratt, H. L., Terry, Y. M., & Van Buren, H. (1998). The impact of an HIV risk-reduction program among street drug users in Rio de Janeiro, Brazil. *American Behavioral Scientist, 41*(8), 1171-1184.

McBride, D., & VanderWaal, C. (1997). Day reporting centers as an alternative for drug using offenders. *Journal of Drug Issues, 27*(2), 379-397.

McBride, D. C., VanderWaal, C., VanBuren, H., & Terry, Y. (1997, November 24). *Breaking the cycle of drug use among juvenile offenders.* Paper prepared for the National Institute of Justice.

Michelsen, T. (1940). Lindesmith's mythology. *Journal of Criminal Law and Criminology, 31*, 373-400.

Mill, J. S. (1921). *On liberty.* Boston: Atlantic Monthly Press.

Moran, R. (1994, April 19). Treatment on demand: The mythology. *Washington Post,* p. A15.

Morganthau, T., Lerner, M. A., Sandza, R., Abbott, N., Gonzalez, D. L., & King, P. (1988, March). The drug gangs. *Newsweek,* pp. 20-27.

Musto, D. F. (1973). *The American disease.* New Haven, CT: Yale University Press.

Nadelmann, E. (1989). Drug prohibition in the United States: Costs, consequences, and alternatives. *Science, 245*, 939-946.

Nadelmann, E., & McNeely, J. (1996). Doing methadone right. *The Public Interest, 123*, 83-93.

National Organization for the Reform of Marijuana Laws (NORML). (1998, Spring). *Who supports medical marijuana? A medical marijuana information guide for state legislators.* Washington, DC: Author.

Needle, R. H., & Coyle, S. L. (1997, February 13). *Community-based outreach risk reduction strategy to prevent HIV-risk behaviors in out-of-treatment injection drug users.* Paper presented at the NIH Consensus Development Conference on Interventions to Prevent HIV Risk Behaviors, National Institute on Drug Abuse, Rockville, MD.

Neighbors. (1988, April 24). *Miami Herald,* pp. 21-25.

Pollan, M. (1997). Living with medical marijuana. *New York Times Magazine, 146*(50859), 22-34.

Price, C. (1996). Putting the harm in harm reduction: Toward a new social policy. *Harm Reduction Communication, 2,* 5.

Public Health Reports. (1997). National drug policy should focus on prevention and treatment. *Public Health Reports, 112*(6), 447-448.

Raab, S. (1988, March 20). The ruthless young crack gangsters. *New York Times,* p. E9.

Rinfret, M. (1988, May 3-4). *Cocaine price, purity, and trafficking trends.* Paper presented at the National Institute on Drug Abuse Technical Review Meeting on the Epidemiology of Cocaine Use and Abuse, Rockville, MD.

Ritzer, G. (1996). *Sociological theory* (4th ed.). New York: McGraw-Hill.

Robinson v. California, 370 U.S. 660 (1962).

Rosenbaum, M. (1996). *Kids, drugs, and drug education: A harm reduction approach* (Policy statement). San Francisco: National Council on Crime and Delinquency.

Rosenbaum, M., Washburn, A., Knight, K., Kelley, M., & Irwin, J. (1996). Treatment as harm reduction, defunding as harm maximization: The case of methadone maintenance. *Journal of Psychoactive Drugs, 28*(3), 241-249.

Rosenbaum, R. (1987, February 15). Crack murder: A detective story. *New York Times Magazine,* pp. 24-33, 57, 60.

Ruche, S. (1995). National Families in Action's twelve reasons not to legalize drugs. Atlanta, GA. National Families in Action.

Savage ride: Buses in a crack zone. (1988, March 7). *Time,* p. 24.

Sisko, B. (1992). Ibogaine update. *Newsletter of the Multidisciplinary Association for Psychedelic Studies (MAPS) 3*(3). http://www.maps.org/news-letters/vO3n3/03319ibo.html accessed 8/18/98.

Sisko, B. (1995). Treatment on demand: Realistic goal or impossible dream? *The Addict Advocate, 3*(1), 1-3.

Stares, P. B. (1996a, June). Drug legalization. *Current,* pp. 383-390.

Stares, P. B. (1996b). Drug legalization? Time for a real debate. *Brookings Review, 14*(2), 18-21.

Stempsey, W. E. (1998). The battle for medical marijuana in the war on drugs. *America, 178*(12), 14-17.

Stephens, R. (1991). *The street addict role.* Albany: State University of New York Press.

Szasz, T. (1996). *Our right to drugs: The case for free market.* Syracuse, NY: Syracuse University Press.

Terry, C., & Pellens, M. (1928). *The opium problem.* New York: Bureau of Social Hygiene.

Trebach, A. S. (1987). *The great drug war.* New York: Macmillan.

Trebach, A. S., & Inciardi, J. A. (1993). *Legalize it? Debating American drug policy.* Washington, DC: American University Press.

U.S. Department of State. (1988, March 1). *International narcotics control strategy report.* Washington, DC: Bureau of International Narcotics Matters, Government Printing Office.

U.S. General Accounting Office. (1987). *Drug smuggling: Large amounts of illegal drugs not seized by federal authorities.* Washington, DC: Government Printing Office.

U.S. General Accounting Office. (1993). *Drug control: Treatment alternatives program for drug offenders needs stronger emphasis.* Washington, DC: Government Printing Office.

United States v. Behrman. 258 U.S. 41, 45 (1922).

Voelker, R. (1997). "Decent research and closure" needed on medical marijuana, says head of NIH panel. *JAMA, 278*(10), 802.

Wilson, J. Q. (1994). What to do about crime. *Commentary, 98,* 25-34.

Wisotsky, S. (1986). *Breaking the impasse in the war on drugs.* New York: Greenwood.

Young, J. H. (1967). *The medical messiahs: A social history of health quackery in twentieth century America.* Princeton, NJ: Princeton University Press.

Legalizing Drugs

Would It Really Reduce Violent Crime?

James A. Inciardi

Frustrated by evidence of only minimal progress in reducing the supply of illegal drugs on the streets of America, and disquieted by media stories of innocent victims of drug-related violence, numerous observers are convinced that the U.S. "War on Drugs" has failed. In an attempt to find a more viable solution to the "drug crisis," or at the very least, to try an alternative strategy, many proposals have been offered. The most controversial of these has been to legalize drugs. The overwhelming majority of Americans, including their political representatives as well as researchers and clinicians working in the drug field consider legalization to be both simplistic and dangerous. By contrast, a small but highly vocal and prestigious minority argue that the benefits of legalizing drugs are well worth the risk.

Since the closing years of the 1980s, an ample body of literature debating drug legalization has accumulated (Nadelmann, 1989; Trebach & Inciardi, 1993; Wilson, 1990). Issues involving crime, public health, ethics, freedom of choice, civil liberties, and public and private harm stir-up healthy discussions. Among these, the crime issue often takes center stage, and the prolegalization group argues that if marijuana, cocaine, heroin, and other drugs were legalized, drug-related crime, and particularly violent crime, would significantly decline (Nadelmann, 1987, 1988a, 1988b, 1988c, 1989; Trebach, 1989, 1990).

By contrast, the antilegalization camps argue that violent crime would not necessarily decline in a legalized drug market and might actually increase for three reasons. First, removing the criminal sanctions against the possession and distribution of illegal drugs would make them more available and attractive and therefore create large numbers of new users. Second, an increase in use would result in a greater number of dysfunctional addicts who could not support themselves, their drug habits, and their drug-taking lifestyles through legitimate means. Hence, crime would be their only alternative. Third, more users would mean more of the violence associated with the ingestion of drugs (Inciardi, McBride, McCoy, Surratt, & Saum, 1995; Kleber, 1994).

These divergent points of view tend to persist because the relationships between drugs and crime are quite complex and because the possible outcomes of a legalized drug market are based primarily on speculation. However, this is an important issue that is not going to go away. As such, the intention here is to review the empirical literature on drugs and violence to determine *what*, if anything, might be inferred from existing data.

■ Considering "Legalization"

How one approaches the legalization/violent crime/increase-decrease quandary depends on how "legalizing drugs" is operationalized. Would all currently illicit drugs be legalized, or would the experiment be limited to just certain ones? True legalization would be akin to selling such drugs as heroin and cocaine on the open market, much like alcohol and tobacco, with a few age-related restrictions. In contrast, there are "medicalization" and "decriminalization" alternatives (Reuben, 1994; Schmoke, 1994). *Medicalization* approaches are of many types, but in essence they would allow users to obtain prescriptions for some, or all, currently illegal substances. *Decriminalization* removes the criminal penalties associated with the possession of small amounts of illegal drugs for personal use while leaving intact the sanctions for trafficking, distribution, and sale.

But, what about *crack*-cocaine? It is clear in the literature that the legalizers, the decriminalizers, and the medicalizers avoid talking about this particular form of cocaine base. Perhaps they do not want to legalize crack out of fear of the drug itself or of public outrage. Arnold Trebach, emeritus professor of law at American University and the former president of the Drug Policy Foundation, is one of the very few who argue for the full legalization of *all* drugs, including crack. However, he explains that most are reluctant to discuss the legalization of crack-cocaine because "it is a very dangerous drug. . . . I know that for many people the very thought of making crack legal destroys any inclination they might have had for even thinking about drug-law reform" (Trebach & Inciardi, 1993, p. 110).

The story of crack is pretty well known, having been reported (and perhaps overreported) in the media since early in 1986—the "highs," binges, and "crashes" that induce addicts to sell their belongings and their bodies in pursuit of more crack; the high addiction liability of the drug that instigates users to commit any manner and variety of crimes to support their habits; the rivalries in crack distribution networks that have turned some inner-city communities into urban "dead zones," where homicide rates are so high that police have written them off as anarchic badlands; the involvement of inner-city youths in the crack business, including the "peewees" and "wanna-bes" (want-to-be's), those street gang acolytes in grade school and junior high school who patrol the streets with walkie-talkies and cellular phones and handguns in the vicinity of crack houses, serving in networks of lookouts, spotters, and steerers, and aspiring to be "rollers" (short for high rollers) in the drug distribution business; and finally, the child abuse, child neglect, and child abandonment by crack-addicted mothers (Chitwood, Rivers, & Inciardi, 1996; Inciardi, Lockwood, & Potteiger, 1993; Ratner, 1993).

There is a related concern associated with the legalization of cocaine. Because crack is easily manufactured from powder cocaine (just add water and baking soda and then cook either on a stove or in a microwave), many drug policy reformers hold that no form of cocaine should be legalized. Logically, this weakens the argument that legalization will reduce drug-related violence, since much of this violence appears to be in the cocaine and crack distribution markets.

Within the context of these remarks, this chapter examines recent empirical studies of drugs and violence in an effort to begin unraveling the legalization/drugs-violence connection. And to better understand the overall relationships between drugs and violence, the analysis makes use of Goldstein's (1985) tripartite conceptual framework of psychopharmacological, economically compulsive, and systemic models of violence.

▪ Psychopharmacological Violence

The common wisdom that violence primarily occurs either when people are desperate for more drugs or as a result of buying and selling drugs and not from the effects of drugs needs to be reconsidered. Users of drugs do get violent when they get high. (Spunt, Brownstein, Goldstein, Fendrich, & Liberty, 1995, pp. 133-134)

The psychopharmacological model of violence suggests that some individuals, as the result of short- or long-term ingestion of specific substances, may become excitable, irrational, and exhibit violent behavior. Research has documented that chronic users of amphetamines, methamphetamine, and cocaine in particular tend to exhibit hostile and aggressive behaviors. Psychopharmacological violence can also be a product of what is known as "cocaine psychosis" (Brody, 1990; Reiss & Roth, 1993; Satel et al., 1991; Weiss & Mirin, 1987, pp. 50-53). As dose and duration of cocaine use increase, the development of cocaine-related psychopathology is not uncommon. Cocaine psychosis is generally preceded by a transitional period characterized by increased suspiciousness, compulsive behavior, fault finding, and eventually paranoia. When the psychotic state is reached, individuals may experience visual and/or auditory hallucinations, with persecutory voices commonly heard. Many believe that they are being followed by police or that family, friends, and others are plotting against them. Moreover, everyday events tend to be misinterpreted in a way that support delusional beliefs. When coupled with the irritability and hyperactivity that the stimulant nature of cocaine tends to generate in almost all of its users, the cocaine-induced paranoia may lead to violent behavior as a means of "self-defense" against imagined persecutors. The violence associated with cocaine psychosis is a common feature in many crack houses across the United States (Inciardi et al., 1993). Violence may also result from the irritability associated with the drug withdrawal syndromes. In addition, some users ingest drugs before committing crimes to both loosen inhibitions and bolster their resolve to break the law (Tunnell, 1992).

Acts of violence may result from either periodic or chronic use of a drug. For example, in a study of drug use and psychopathy among Baltimore city jail inmates, researchers at the University of Baltimore reported that cocaine use was related to assault, irritability, resentment, and hostility and concluded that these indicators of aggression may be a function of *drug effects* rather than predisposing conditions (Fishbein & Reuland, 1994). Similarly, Barry Spunt and his colleagues at National Development and Research Institutes (NDRI) in New York City found that of 269 convicted murderers incarcerated in New York State prisons 45% were high at the time of the offense (Spunt et al., 1995). Three in 10 believed the homicide was related to their drug use, challenging conventional beliefs that violence only infrequently occurs as a result of the effects of drug consumption. Even marijuana, which prolegalizers consider harmless, may have a connection with violence and crime. Spunt, Goldstein, Brownstein, and Fendrich (1994) and his colleagues also attempted to determine the role of marijuana in the crimes of the homicide offenders they interviewed in the New York State prisons. One third of those who had ever used marijuana had smoked the drug in the 24-hour period prior to the homicide. Moreover, 31% of those who considered themselves to be "high" at the time of committing murder felt that the homicide and marijuana were related. It might be added here that William Blount of the University of South Florida interviewed abused women in prisons and shelters for battered women located throughout Florida. He and his colleagues found that

24% of those who killed their abusers were marijuana users while only 8% of those who did not kill their abusers smoked marijuana (Blount, Silverman, Sellers, & Seese, 1994).

In an alternative direction, a point that needs to be emphasized here is that alcohol is linked with violence to a far greater extent than any illegal drug (Miczek et al., 1994; Murdoch, Pihl, & Ross, 1990). For most addicts, the drug of choice is alcohol—because it is both legal (and therefore accessible) and inexpensive in comparison to other drugs. The extent to which alcohol claims responsibility for violent crimes compared with other drugs is apparent when the statistics are examined. For example, Carolyn Block and her colleagues at the Criminal Justice Information Authority in Chicago found that between 1982 and 1989, the use of alcohol by offenders or victims in local homicides ranged from 18% to 32% (Block, Wilson, & Daly, 1990).

Alcohol appears quite able to reduce the inhibitory control of threat, making it more likely that a person will exhibit behaviors normally suppressed by fear. In turn, this reduction of inhibition heightens the probability that intoxicated persons will perpetrate, or become victims of, aggressive behavior (Pihl, Peterson, & Lau, 1993). In this regard, consider the following comment by an anonymous physician, on the relationship between alcohol and crime: "When I see lung cancer, I'm 95% certain that cigarettes are involved; when I see a stab wound, I'm just as sure that alcohol is involved" (in Benjamin & Miller, 1991, p. 109).

A second physician, the director of emergency care at a major metropolitan hospital, was even more emphatic, stating "I have never seen a stab wound in which alcohol was not involved."

Backing up these anecdotal accounts, Douglass Murdoch of Quebec's McGill University found that in some 9,000 criminal cases drawn from a multinational sample 62% of violent offenders were drinking shortly before or at the time of the offense (Murdoch et al., 1990). A more recent study by researchers at the School of Public Health at the University of Texas-Houston surveyed 2,075 ninth- and 11th-grade students in a large Texas school district. Their purpose was to examine the co-morbidity of violence and health risk behaviors. Findings indicated that male students involved in fighting and carrying weapons were almost 20 times more likely to drink alcohol regularly than those who were less aggressive (Orpinas, Basen-Engquist, Grunbaum, & Parcel, 1995).

Alcohol has consistently been linked to homicide. NDRI's Barry Spunt and his colleagues (Spunt, Goldstein, Brownstein, Fendrich, & Langley, 1994) interviewed 268 homicide offenders incarcerated in New York State correctional facilities to determine the role of alcohol in their crimes. Of the respondents, 31% reported being drunk at the time of the crime and 19% believed the homicide was related to their drinking. Similarly, in Blount et al.'s (1994) study of abused women in Florida, it was found that those women who eventually killed their abusers were more likely to use alcohol (64%) than those who did not (44%).

Substance use by violent offenders is often apparent to the victims of violence. For example, the U.S. Department of Justice (1992) found that 21% of victims of violent crimes believed their offender to have been under the influence of alcohol, and 7.6% believed other drugs influenced the offender's behavior. Similarly, in a study of urban violence, medical records and interviews of patients entering a small city trauma center in Youngstown, Ohio, determined that the victims considered their attackers to have been under the influence of alcohol and/or other drugs in 60% of the cases (Buss, Abdu, & Walker, 1995).

When analyzing the psychopharmacological model of drugs and violence, most of the discussions focus on the offender and the role of drugs in causing or facilitating crime. But what about the victims? Are the victims of drug- and alcohol-related homicides simply casualties of someone else's substance abuse? In addressing these questions, the data document that victims are likely to be drug users as well. For example, based on an analysis of the 4,298 homicides that occurred in New York City during 1990 and 1991, Kenneth Tardiff of Cornell University Medical College found that the victims of these offenses were 10 to 50 times more likely to be cocaine users than were members of the general population (Tardiff et al., 1994). Of the White female victims, 60% in the 25-34 age group had cocaine in their systems; for Black females the figure increased to 72%. Tardiff speculated that the classic symptoms of cocaine use—irritability, paranoia, or aggressiveness—may have instigated the violence. In another study of cocaine users in New York City, it was found that female high-volume users were victims of violence far more frequently than low-volume users and nonusers of cocaine (Goldstein, Bellucci, Spunt, & Miller, 1991). Studies in numerous other cities and countries have yielded the same general findings—that a great many of the victims of homicide and other forms of violence are drinkers and drug users themselves (Collins, 1981).

An aspect of the drugs/violence connection rarely mentioned as part of the psychopharmacological model is driving while under the influence (DUI) of alcohol or other drugs. According to a 1997 National Highway Traffic Safety Administration report, alcohol was involved in nearly 39% of all fatal motor vehicle crashes. Moreover, data from the Centers for Disease Control (1997) indicate that alcohol is involved in nearly 25% of motor vehicle-related deaths among children aged 15 and under. As for driving under the influence of illegal drugs, data suggest that it is not uncommon. For example, in a Memphis, Tennessee, study of persons arrested for reckless driving who did not appear to be under the influence of alcohol, urinalysis tests found 58% to be positive for cocaine, marijuana, or both (Brookoff, Cook, Williams, & Mann, 1994).

■ Economically Compulsive Violence

The economically compulsive model of violence holds that some drug users engage in economically oriented violent crime to support drug use. This model is illustrated in the many studies of drug use and criminal behavior that demonstrate that, although drug sales, property crimes, and prostitution are the primary economic offenses committed by users, armed robberies and muggings do indeed occur (Fagan & Chin, 1991; Inciardi, 1986, 1992).

Analyzing the legalization/drugs-violence connection within this model is far more complex than with the psychopharmacological pattern. The contention is that in a legalized market the prices of "expensive drugs" would decline to more affordable levels and hence predatory crimes would become unnecessary. This argument is based on several premises. First, it assumes that there is empirical support for what has been referred to as the "enslavement theory of addiction." Second, it assumes that people addicted to drugs commit crimes only for the purpose of supporting their habits. Third, it assumes that in a legalized market users could obtain as much of the drugs as they wanted whenever they wanted. Finally, it assumes that if drugs are inexpensive they will be affordable and hence crime will be unnecessary.

With respect to the first premise, for the better part of this century there has been a concerted belief that addicts commit crimes because they are "enslaved" to drugs, that because of the high prices of heroin, cocaine, and other illicit chemicals on the drug black market, users are forced to commit crimes in order to support their drug habits. Interestingly, however, there is no solid empirical evidence to support this contention. From the 1920s through the close of the 1960s, hundreds of studies of the relationship between crime and addiction were conducted (Austin & Lettieri, 1976; Greenberg & Adler, 1974). Invariably, when one analysis would support the posture of "enslavement theory," the next would affirm the view that addicts were criminals first and that their drug use was but one more manifestation of their deviant lifestyles. In retrospect, the difficulty lay in the ways that many of the studies had been conducted, with biases and deficiencies in research designs and sampling that rendered their findings of little value.

Research since the middle of the 1970s with active drug users on the streets of New York, Miami, Baltimore, and elsewhere has demonstrated that enslavement theory has little basis in reality (Inciardi, 1986, pp. 115-143; Johnson et al., 1985; McBride & McCoy, 1982; Nurco , Ball, Shaffer, & Hanlon, 1985; Stephens & McBride, 1976). All of these studies of the criminal careers of heroin, cocaine, and other drug users have convincingly documented that although drug use tends to intensify and perpetuate criminal behavior it usually does not initiate criminal careers. In fact, the evidence suggests that among the majority of street drug users involved in crime their criminal careers were well established prior to the onset of either narcotics or cocaine use. As such, it would appear that the "inference of causality"—that the high price of drugs on the black market per se causes crime—is simply not supported.

Looking at the second premise, a variety of studies document that drug use is not the only reason why addicts commit predatory crimes. They also do so to support their daily living expenses—food, clothing, and shelter. To cite but one example, researchers at the Center for Drug and Alcohol Studies at the University of Delaware studied crack users on the streets of Miami. Of the scores of active

addicts interviewed, 85% of the men and 70% of the women paid
for portions of their living expenses through street crime. In fact,
half of the men and one fourth of the women paid for 90% or more
of their living expenses through crime. And not surprisingly, 96%
of the men and 99% of the women had not held a legal job in the
90-day period before being interviewed for the study (Inciardi &
Pottieger, 1994).

With respect to the third premise, that in a legalized market users
could obtain as much of the drugs as they wanted whenever they
wanted, only speculation is possible. More than likely there would be
some sort of regulation, and hence drug black markets would persist
for those whose addictions were beyond the medicalized or legalized
allotments. In a decriminalized market, levels of drug-related violence
would likely either remain unchanged or increase (if drug use increased).

As for the last premise, that cheap drugs preclude the need to
commit crimes to obtain them, the evidence emphatically suggests
that this is not at all the case. Consider crack-cocaine. Although
crack "rocks" are available on the illegal market for as little as $2 in
some locales, users are still involved in crime-driven endeavors to
support their addictions. For example, Miller and Gold (1994) surveyed 200 consecutive callers to the 1-800-COCAINE hotline who
considered themselves to have a problem with crack. The researchers
found that, despite the low cost of crack, 63% of daily users and 40%
of nondaily users spent more than $200 per week on the drug.
Similarly, interviews conducted by NDRI researchers in New York
City with almost 400 drug users contacted in the streets, jails, and
treatment programs found that almost half spent over $1,000 a
month on crack (Johnson, Natarajan, Dunlap, & Elmoghazy, 1994).
The study also documented that crack users—despite the low cost of
their drug of choice—spent more money on drugs than did users of
heroin, powder cocaine, marijuana, and alcohol.

Miller and Gold (1994) summarized the issue of crack and crime
by stating "Once the severity of addictive use is established, the
pattern of the cost of maintaining the addiction and its consequences
is related to preoccupation with acquisition and compulsive use"
(p. 1075).

■ Systemic Violence

The systemic model of violence maintains that violent crime is intrinsic to the very involvement with illicit substances. As such, systemic violence refers to the traditionally aggressive patterns of interaction within systems of illegal drug trafficking and distribution. It is the systemic violence associated with trafficking in cocaine and crack in America's inner cities that has brought the most attention to drug-related violence in recent years. Moreover, it is concerns with this same violence that has focused the current interest on the possibility of legalizing drugs. And it is certainly logical to assume that if heroin and cocaine were legal substances systemic drug-related violence might indeed decline significantly. However, there are two very important questions in this regard. First, is drug-related violence more often psychopharmacological than systemic? Second, is the great bulk of systemic violence related to the distribution of crack? If most of the drug-related violence is psychopharmacological in nature, and if systemic violence is typically related to crack—the drug generally excluded from consideration when legalization is argued—then it might be logical to conclude that legalizing drugs would *not* reduce violent crime.

Evidence from studies in New York City tend to contradict, or at least fail to support, the notion that legalizing drugs would reduce violent, systemic-related crime. For example, Goldstein et al.'s (1991) ethnographic studies of male and female drug users during the late 1980s found that cocaine-related violence was more often psychopharmacological than systemic. Among men, the greater the volume of cocaine consumed, the more violence they engaged in—most of which was unrelated to cocaine sales or distribution. Among the women, the great majority of violent events in which they were involved were not drug related.

Similarly, in the study of 4,298 New York City homicides mentioned earlier, 31% of the victims had used cocaine in the 24-hour period prior to their deaths (Tardiff et al., 1994). One of the conclusions of the study was that the homicides were not necessarily related to drug dealing. In all likelihood, as victims of homicide, the cocaine users may have provoked violence through irritability, paranoid thinking, and verbal or physical aggression—all of which are known to be among the psychopharmacological effects of cocaine.

Shifting to the alternative consideration, in a 1988 study of 414 New York City homicide events, 47% were not drug related, 10% were alcohol related, and the remaining 43% involved illegal drugs (Goldstein, Brownstein, Ryan, & Bellucci, 1989). Interestingly, 60% of the drug-related homicides involved crack, and as noted earlier, those arguing for legalizing drugs retreat from increasing the availability of crack. Going further, another 10% of the drug-related homicides were alcohol related. Thus, if alcohol, crack, and non-drug-related homicides were removed from consideration, only 87 homicides remain, or 21% of the total that potentially could have been eliminated if drugs were legal. And that is New York City, where drug use and violence rates were among the highest at the time of the study.

Going beyond this issue, there is another important question. Is all of the systemic violence we see in the drug industry actually drug-related? Some of it may be only indirectly related or not at all (Inciardi et al., 1995; Reiss & Roth, 1993). In Goldstein et al.'s (1991) study of high volume cocaine users, it was suggested that drug use may be a symptom of a mode of living that includes violence that is not directly related to cocaine use or distribution. "Indirect" violence in the drug marketplace ranges from weapons readily accessible during disputes over nondrug matters, armed robberies targeting buyers carrying money and sellers transporting drugs, and female buyers who became victims of sexual assault (Reiss & Roth, 1993). Ansley Hamid (1990), a noted researcher and professor at John Jay College of Criminal Justice, made a striking point in this regard:

> Even among youth who are not crack users or distributors, crack continues to stimulate violence. The model it so vividly presents—extreme youth in control, adults "out of control," women exploited, the short life glorified—apparently absorbs whole neighborhoods faster than crack itself can addict. (p. 67)

A related issue is that guns contribute to violence both inside and outside the drug marketplace. In fact, firearm violence may be less related to the drug trade than is popularly believed. In a study of drug involvement and firearms possession by juveniles, Joseph Sheley of Tulane University found in 1994 that gun activity did not increase with rises in levels of drug use. Self-administered question-naires given to over 800 male inmates in reform schools of four states (California, New Jersey, Illinois, and Louisiana) revealed that 83% had owned a gun prior to confinement and 69% owned three or more guns. Although 47% had used illicit drugs in the year or two before confinement and 25% were considered heavy users, nondrug users were equally as likely as users to possess, carry, and fire a gun. However, when broken down by sellers and nonsellers of drugs, a relationship emerged—those who sold drugs were more likely to possess, carry, and fire a gun. This certainly demonstrates a link between drug selling and firearm violence (though not necessarily a causal link), but it also shows that nonusers and nondealers are also heavily involved in gun activity.

There is evidence that the drive-by shootings that occur in our nation's inner cities have little or nothing to do with drugs. For example, in Lawrence Sherman's study in 1988 of shootings of inno-cent bystanders in four large cities, such shootings accounted for less than 1% of all homicides, and drug market conflicts were only one of several causes of the shootings (Sherman, Steele, Laufersweiler, Hoffer, & Julian, 1989). In a study of children and adolescents injured or killed in drive-by shootings in Los Angeles, investigators deter-mined that those at risk for firearm violence lived in areas where gang rivalry and retaliatory shootings were frequent and that drug traffick-ing was not believed to be a major causative factor (Hutson, Anglin, & Pratts, 1994).

Research with gangs has also shown that lethal street violence is more often related to intergang battles over territory and other factors unrelated to the drug trade. In their study of 288 gang-related homicides in Chicago from 1987 through 1990, Carolyn and Richard Block (1993) found that less than 3% of the killings were drug related. Similar findings can be seen in studies by Klein, Maxson, and Cunningham (1991) at the University of Southern California. After analyzing 3 years' worth of narcotics and homicide files at the Los Angeles Police and County Sheriff's departments, they concluded that there was only a weak association between street gangs, drug distribution, and violence. Most interesting, they found that gang violence— including homicide—did not increase with the introduc-tion and proliferation of crack-cocaine in the mid-1980s. A subse-quent study by researchers from the Centers for Disease Control came to the same conclusion—that gang violence in Los Angeles was typically unrelated to drugs (Meehan & O'Carroll, 1992). And finally, in a study of gang-related homicides published in the *Journal of the American Medical Association* towards the close of 1995 there was a similar conclusion (Houston, Anglin, Kyriacou, Hart, & Spears, 1995). Of the 7,288 gang-related homicides that occurred in Los Angeles County from 1979 through 1994, drug trafficking was not considered a major factor. Rather, the problems were the increasing numbers of violent street gangs and gang members, greater levels of intergang violence, an increase in the use of firearms in gang violence, worsening socioeconomic conditions in the inner city, and the continual breakdown of sociocultural institutions.

■ Discussion

Study after study document that alcohol and other drugs have psychopharmacological effects that result in violence. Cocaine in all of its forms is linked to aggressive behavior as a result of the irritability and paranoia it engenders. Also, alcohol and cocaine have been found to be present in both the perpetrators and victims of violence. Alcohol is legal and cocaine is not, suggesting that the legal status of a drug may be unrelated to the issue of psychopharmacological violence. Hence, it is unlikely that such violence would decline if drugs were legalized.

Studies of economically compulsive violence also suggest that in a legalized market, crime would not necessarily decline. Users who engage in predatory behaviors do so for a variety of reasons—not only to obtain drugs but also to support themselves. And typically, as many studies suggest, drug-involved offenders were crime involved before the onset of their careers in drugs. Too, even when a drug is inexpensive, it still may not be affordable if there is addiction and compulsive use. This is amply illustrated in the experience with crack.

As for systemic violence, much of it is unrelated to the use of drugs. When it *is* drug linked, the overwhelming majority of violent episodes seems to be associated with the use of alcohol or crack, and this brings us to another interesting consideration. The illegal drug most associated with systemic violence is crack-cocaine, and of all illicit drugs, crack is the one now responsible for the most homicides.

In a study done in New York City in 1988 by Goldstein and his colleagues, crack was found to be connected to 32% of all homicides and 60% of all drug-related homicides. What they concluded was that crack-related homicides appeared to be replacing other forms of homicide rather than augmenting the existing homicide rate.

Taking this point further, violence stems from many of the dysfunctional aspects of our society other than drug use. After studying the violence associated with crack distribution in Manhattan neighborhoods, Fagan and Chin (1990) concluded that crack has been integrated into behaviors that were evident before drug sellers' involvement with crack or its appearance on New York City streets. In other words, the crack users/dealers of today are often engrossed in violent and crime-involved lifestyles that likely exist (and previously did) independent of their involvement with crack. Furthermore, although there is evidence that crack sellers are more violent than other drug sellers, this violence is not confined to the drug-selling context—violence potentials appear to precede involvement in selling (Fagan & Chin, 1990).

It appears, then, that crack has been blamed for increasing violence in the marketplace, but perhaps this violence actually stems from the psychopharmacological consequences of crack use. *Crack dealers* are generally *crack users*, and since crack is highly addictive yet comparatively inexpensive, there is a continuous demand for it. This leads to the competition that generates violence. Legalizing crack would likely reduce the competition but increase the demand. Hamid (1990) reasons that increases in crack-related violence are due to the deterioration of informal and formal social controls throughout communities that have been destabilized by economic processes and political decisions. As such, does anyone really believe that we can improve on these complex social problems through the simple act of legalizing drugs?

As a final point here, the issue of whether or not legalization would create a multitude of new users needs to be addressed. This is important because it is at the heart of the argument of those who oppose legalization, and on this there are three issues. First, many biologists and anthropologists have argued that people have an inborn drive to alter their normal states of consciousness (Tiger, 1992; Weil, 1972). If the illicit drugs were suddenly legal, would the many who are currently suppressing this desire to experience an altered state give in to it? Second, many people do not use drugs simply because they are illegal. Or as Mark Kleiman (1992), author of *Against Excess: Drug Policy for Results*, recently put it,

> Illegality by itself tends to suppress consumption, independent of its effect on price, both because some consumers are reluctant to disobey the law and because illegal products are harder to find and less reliable as to quality and labeling than legal ones. (p. 108)

And third, although there is no way of accurately estimating how many new users there would be if drugs were legalized, in all likelihood there would be many. Currently, relatively few people are steady users of drugs. The University of Michigan's Monitoring the Future study for 1997 reported that less than 1% of high school seniors are daily users of either hallucinogens, cocaine, heroin, sedatives, or inhalants (Johnston, O'Malley, & Bachman, 1998). In fact, it is the addicts who overwhelmingly consume the bulk of the drug supply— 80% of all alcohol and almost 100% of all heroin (Benjamin & Miller, 1991). In other words, there are significantly large numbers of non-users who have yet to even try drugs, let alone use them regularly. Of those who begin to use drugs "recreationally," researchers estimate that approximately 10% go on to serious, heavy, chronic, compulsive use (Grabowski, 1984). Herbert Kleber, former deputy director of the Office of National Drug Control Policy, estimated that cocaine users might increase from the current 2 million to between 18 and 50 million— which are the estimated numbers of problem drinkers and nicotine addicts (Kleber, 1994).

Restrictions on alcohol have curtailed its widespread usage. During Prohibition, there was a decrease of 20% to 50% in the number of practicing alcoholics. These estimates were calculated based on a decline in cirrhosis and other alcohol-related deaths (Jellinek, 1960). After Prohibition ended, both of these indicators increased. More recently, when the drinking age was raised from age 18 to 21 across the United States, deaths from drinking and driving decreased dramatically.

What all of this suggests is that drug prohibition seems to be having some very positive effects and that legalizing drugs would not necessarily have a depressant effect on violent crime. With legalization, violent crime would likely escalate; or perhaps, some types of systemic violence would decline at the expense of greatly increasing the overall rate of violent crime. Moreover, legalizing drugs would likely increase physical illnesses and compound any existing psychiatric problems among users and their family members. And finally, legalizing drugs would not eliminate the effects of unemployment, inadequate housing, deficient job skills, economic worries, and physical abuse that typically contribute to the use of drugs.

References

Austin, G. A., & Lettieri, D. J. (1976). *Drugs and crime: The relationship of drug use and concomitant criminal behavior.* Rockville, MD: National Institute on Drug Abuse.

Benjamin, D. K., & Miller, R. L. (1991). *Undoing drugs: Beyond legalization.* New York: Basic Books.

Block, C. R., & Block, R. L. (1993, December). *Street gang crime in Chicago.* Washington, DC: U.S. Department of Justice.

Block, C. R., Block, R. L., Wilson, M., & Daly, M. (1990, November 5). *Chicago homicide from the sixties to the nineties: Have patterns of lethal violence changed?* Paper presented at the annual meeting of the American Society of Criminology, Baltimore, MD.

Blount, W. R., Silverman, I. J., Sellers, C. S., & Seese, R. A. (1994, Spring). Alcohol and drug use among abused women who kill, abused women who don't, and their abusers. *Journal of Drug Issues*, pp. 166-177.

Brody, S. L. (1990). Violence associated with acute cocaine use in patients admitted to a medical emergency department. In M. De La Rosa, E. Y. Lambert, & B. Gropper (Eds.), *Drugs and violence: Causes, correlates, and consequences* (Monograph No. 103, DHHS Pub. No. ADM 90-1721). Rockville, MD: National Institute on Drug Abuse.

Brookoff, D., Cook, C. S., Williams, C., & Mann, C. S. (1994, August 25). Testing reckless drivers for cocaine and marijuana. *New England Journal of Medicine, 331*, 518-522.

Buss, T. F., Abdu, R., & Walker, J. R. (1995). Alcohol, drugs, and urban violence in a small city trauma center. *Journal of Substance Abuse Treatment, 12*(2), 75-83.

Centers for Disease Control. (1997). Alcohol-related traffic fatalities involving children—United States, 1985-1996. *Morbidity and Mortality Weekly Report, 46* (48), 1129-1133.

Chitwood, D. D., Rivers, J. E., & Inciardi, J. A. (1996). *The American pipe dream: Crack and the inner city.* Fort Worth, TX: Harcourt Brace.

Collins, J. J. (Ed.). (1981). *Drinking and crime.* New York: Guilford.

Fagan, J., & Chin, K. (1990). Violence as regulation and social control in the distribution of crack. In M. De La Rosa, E. Y. Lambert, & B. Gropper (Eds.), *Drugs and violence: Causes, correlates, and consequences* (Monograph No. 103, DHSS Pub. No. ADM 90-1721). Rockville, MD: National Institute on Drug Abuse.

Fagan, J., & Chin, K. (1991). Social processes of initiation into crack. *Journal of Drug Issues, 21*, 313-343.

Fishbein, D. H., & Reuland, M. (1994). Psychological correlates of frequency and type of drug use among jail inmates. *Addictive Behaviors, 19*(6), 583-598.

Goldstein, P. J. (1985). Drugs and violent behavior. *Journal of Drug Issues, 15*, 493-506.

Goldstein, P. J., Brownstein, H. H., Ryan, P. J., & Bellucci, P. A. (1989). Crack and homicide in New York City, 1988: A conceptually based event analysis. *Contemporary Drug Problems, 16*, 651-687.

Goldstein, P. J., Bellucci, P. A., Spunt, B. J., & Miller, T. (1991). Volume of cocaine use and violence: A comparison between men and women. *Journal of Drug Issues, 21*, 345-367.

Grabowski, J. (Ed.). (1984). *Cocaine: Pharmacology, effects and treatment of abuse.* Rockville, MD: National Institute on Drug Abuse.

Greenberg, S. W., & Adler, F. (1974). Crime and addiction: An empirical analysis of the literature, 1920-1973. *Contemporary Drug Problems, 3*, 221-270.

Hamid, A. (1990, Spring). The political economy of crack related violence. *Contemporary Drug Problems*, pp. 31-78.

Houston, H. R., Anglin, D., Kyriacou, D. N., Hart, J., & Spears, K. (1995, October 4). The epidemic of gang-related homicides in Los Angeles County from 1979 through 1994. *Journal of the American Medical Association, 274*(13), 1031(6).

Hutson, H. R., Anglin, D., & Pratts Jr., M. J. (1994). Adolescents and children injured or killed in drive-by shootings. *The New England Journal of Medicine, 330*, 324-327.

Inciardi, J. A. (1986). *The war on drugs: Heroin, cocaine, crime, and public policy.* Mountain View, CA: Mayfield.

Inciardi, J. A. (1992). *The war on drugs II: The continuing epic of heroin, cocaine, crack, crime, AIDS, and public policy.* Mountain View, CA: Mayfield.

Inciardi, J. A., Lockwood, D., & Pottieger, A. E. (1993). *Women and crack-cocaine.* New York: Macmillan.

Inciardi, J. A., McBride, D. C., McCoy, C. B., Surratt, H. L., & Saum, C. A. (1995). Violence, street crime and the drug legalization debate: A perspective and commentary on the U.S. experience. *Studies on Crime and Crime Prevention, 4*(1), 105-118.

Inciardi, J. A., & Pottieger, A. E. (1994). Crack cocaine use and street crime. *Journal of Drug Issues, 24*(2), 273-292.

Jellinek, E. M. (1960). *The disease concept of alcoholism.* New Haven, CT: Hillhouse Press.

Johnson, B. D., Goldstein, P. J., Preble, E., Schmeidler, J., Lipton, D. S., Spunt, B., & Miller, T. (1985). *Taking care of business: The economics of crime by heroin users.* Lexington, MA: Lexington Books.

Johnson, B. D., Natarajan, M., Dunlap, E., & Elmoghazy, E. (1994). Crack abusers and noncrack abusers: Profiles of drug use, drug sales and nondrug criminality. *Journal of Drug Issues, 24*(1), 117-141.

Johnston, L. D., O'Malley, P. M., & Bachman, J. G. (1998). *Monitoring the future, 1997*. Ann Arbor: University of Michigan Press.

Kleber, H. (1994). Our current approach to drug abuse-Progress, problems, proposals. *New England Journal of Medicine, 330*, 361-365.

Klein, M. W., Maxson, C. L., & Cunningham, L. C. (1991). "Crack," street gangs, and violence. *Criminology, 29*(4), 623-650.

Kleiman, M. A. R. (1992). *Against excess: Drug policy for results*. New York: Basic Books.

McBride, D. C., Burgman-Habermehl, C., Alpert, J., & Chitwood, D. D. (1986). Drugs and homicide. *Bulletin of the New York Academy of Medicine, 62*(5), 497-508.

McBride, D. C., & McCoy, C. B. (1982, Spring). Crime and drugs: The issues and the literature. *Journal of Drug Issues, 12*, 137-152.

Meehan, P. J., & O'Carroll, P. W. (1992). Gangs, drugs, and homicide in Los Angeles. *American Journal of Disadvantaged Children, 146*(6), 683-687.

Miczek, K. A., DeBold, J. F., Haney, M., Tidey, J., Vivian, J., & Weerts, E. M. (1994). Alcohol, drugs of abuse, aggression, and violence. In A. J. Reiss, Jr., & J. Roth (Eds.), *Understanding and preventing violence:* Vol. 3. Societal influences (pp. 377-570). Washington, DC: National Academy Press.

Miller, N., & Gold, M. (1994). Criminal activity and crack addiction. *International Journal of the Addictions, 29*(8), 1069-1078.

Murdoch, D., Pihl, R. O., & Ross, D. (1990). Alcohol and crimes of violence: Present issues. *International Journal of the Addictions, 25*, 1065-1081.

Nadelmann, E. A. (1987, June 2). *The real international drug problem*. Paper presented at the Defense Academic Research Support Conference "International Drugs: Threat and Response." National Defense College, Defense Intelligence Analysis Center, Washington, DC.

Nadelmann, E. A. (1988a). The case for legalization. *Public Interest, 92*, 3-31.

Nadelmann, E. A. (1988b). U.S. drug policy: A bad export. *Foreign Policy, 70*, 83-108.

Nadelmann, E. A. (1988c, September 29). *Legalization of illicit drugs: Impact and feasibility*. Select Committee Hearing on Narcotics Abuse and Control, House of Representatives, 100th Congress, Washington, DC.

Nadelmann, E. A. (1989). Drug prohibition in the United States: Cost, consequences, and alternatives. *Science, 245*, 939-947.

National Highway Traffic Safety Administration. (1998). *Traffic safety facts 1997*. Washington, DC: National Center for Statistics and Analysis, U.S. Department of Treasury.

Nurco, D. N., Ball, J. C., Shaffer, J. W., & Hanlon, T. F. (1985). The criminality of narcotic addicts. *Journal of Nervous and Mental Disease, 173*, 94-102.

Orpinas, P. K., Basen-Engquist, K., Grunbaum, J., & Parcel, G. S. (1995). The co-morbidity of violence-related behaviors with health-risk behaviors in a population of high school students. *Journal of Adolescent Health, 16*, 216-225.

Pihl, R. O., Peterson, J. B., & Lau, M. A. (1993, September). A biosocial model of the alcohol-aggression relationship. *Journal of Studies on Alcohol, 11*, 128-139.

Ratner, M. (1993). *Crack pipe as pimp: An ethnographic investigation of sex-for-crack exchanges*. New York: Lexington Books.

Reiss, A. J., & Roth, J. (Eds.). (1993). *Understanding and preventing violence: Vol. 3. Societal Influences.* Washington, DC: National Academy Press.

Reuben, R. C. (1994). New president willing to speak up: Media takes note of Bushnell's drug policy comments. *ABA Journal, 80,* 85.

Satel, S. L., Price, L. H., Palumbo, J. M., McDougle, C. J., Krystal, J. H., Gawin, F., Charney, D. S., Heninger, G. R., & Kleber, H. D. (1991, December). Clinical phenomenology and neurobiology of cocaine abstinence: A prospective inpatient study. *American Journal of Psychiatry, 148,* 1712-1716.

Schmoke, K. L. (1994, May 5). Side effects. *Rolling Stone, 38*(2).

Sheley, J. F. (1994). Drug activity and firearms possession and use by juveniles. *Journal of Drug Issues, 24*(3), 363-382.

Sherman, L. W., Steele, L., Laufersweiler, D., Hoffer, N., & Julian, S. A. (1989). Stray bullets and "mushrooms": Random shootings of bystanders in four cities, 1977-1988. *Journal of Quantitative Criminology, 5*(4), 297-316.

Spunt, B., Brownstein, H., Goldstein, P., Fendrich, M., & Liberty, H. J. (1995). Drug use by homicide offenders. *Journal of Psychoactive Drugs, 27*(2), 125-134.

Spunt, B., Goldstein, P., Brownstein, H., & Fendrich, M. (1994). The role of marijuana in homicide. *International Journal of the Addictions, 29*(2), 195-213.

Spunt, B., Goldstein, P., Brownstein, H., Fendrich, M., & Langley, S. (1994). Alcohol and homicide: Interviews with prison inmates. *Journal of Drug Issues, 24*(1), 143-163.

Stephens, R. C., & McBride, D. C. (1976). Becoming a street addict. *Human Organization, 35,* 87-93.

Tardiff, K., Marzuk, P. M., Leon, A. C., Hirsch, C. S., Stajic, M., Portera, L., & Hartwell, N. (1994). Homicide in New York City: Cocaine use and firearms. *Journal of the American Medical Association, 272*(1), 43-46.

Tiger, L. (1992). *The pursuit of pleasure.* Boston: Little, Brown.

Trebach, A. S. (1989). Tough choices: The practical politics of drug policy reform. *American Behavioral Scientist, 32,* 249-258.

Trebach, A. S. (1990). A bundle of peaceful compromises. *Journal of Drug Issues, 20,* 515-531.

Trebach, A. S., & Inciardi, J. A. (1993). *Legalize it? Debating American drug policy.* Washington, DC: American University Press.

Tunnell, K. D. (1992). *Choosing crime: The criminal calculus of property offenders.* Chicago: Nelson-Hall.

U.S. Department of Justice, Bureau of Justice Statistics. (1992). *Drugs and crime facts, 1991.* Washington, DC: Government Printing Office.

Weil, A. (1972). *The natural mind: A new way of looking at drugs and the higher consciousness.* Boston: Houghton Mifflin.

Weiss, R. D., & Mirin, S. M. (1987). *Cocaine.* Washington, DC: American Psychiatric Press.

Wilson, J. Q. (1990, February). Against the legalization of drugs. *Commentary,* pp. 21-28.

The Marijuana Legalization Debate

Is There a Middle Ground?

MICHAEL L. DENNIS
WILLIAM WHITE

The legalization debate today is very different from when it began with the hearings for the Marijuana Tax Act of 1937 that effectively made it illegal through high taxation. In the 17 years prior to the Act, only seven articles were listed in the *Reader's Guide to Periodic Literature* and the main concerns expressed at the time were

AUTHORS' NOTE: The authors acknowledge funding from the Center for Substance Abuse Treatment Coordinating Center Grant (1 UR4 TI11320-01), useful comments from Peter Bergstrom, Randall Webber, and an anonymous reviewer, and assistance from Joan Unsicker, Joyce Thomas, and Amelia Goembel in preparing the manuscript. The opinions expressed in this chapter are solely those of the authors and do not reflect official positions of the government.

that (1) farmers would be inconvenienced by having to kill a plant that grew wild in many parts of the country, (2) domestic hemp industries would be damaged, (3) paint and varnish companies would have to find a new source of oil (then obtained from hemp seeds), and (4) impact of having to remove hemp from bird seed on "singing birds" (Bonnie & Whitebread, 1970). Most of the information presented against marijuana was hearsay about how it turned people into murderers and would be used by the underworld to enslave youths, or it was tinged with anti-Hispanic tones about migrant workers (Sloman, 1979). In the ensuing years, there has been a near continuous and highly polarized debate concerning marijuana. Policy arguments have and often continue to be framed at the extremes of draconian prohibition/criminalization, on the one side, and unfettered legalization/miracle cure plant promotion, on the other. Today, marijuana is both the most commonly used illicit drug (suggesting that many people do not agree with or care about the risks) and, for adolescents, the illegal drug most likely to be mentioned in arrests, emergency room admissions, and autopsy reports (suggesting that it is not the harmless substance proclaimed by its proponents). In this chapter, we attempt to contrast the major arguments being made by both sides and explore whether there is any middle ground in the continuing debate over the legal status of marijuana in the United States.

■ Themes Around Which the Debate and This Chapter Are Organized

Even a cursory review of marijuana policy discussions leads to the conclusion that this is a debate of extremes: soft versus hard drugs, good versus bad drugs, supply reduction versus demand reduction, miracle drug versus carcinogenic, prohibition versus legalization. It is also apparent that the debate is often conducted with code words that say as much about issues of social class, race, gender, generation, and institutional self-interest than about drugs and drug policies. Complicating matters further, both sides of the debate consider the status quo unacceptable and seem to use some of the same data to reach radically different conclusions. Table 4.1 provides a summary of some of the main themes in the debate and highlights some of the arguments being made on both sides. The chapter is organized according to these themes, and in each section we attempt to summarize the argument on each side and then present our understanding of the middle ground. Taking all of the information together, in the final section we summarize the implications for policymakers and present our recommendations.

Right to Use

One of the most fundamental concepts for the proponents of legalization is the idea that individuals should have the right to decide whether to use marijuana just like cigarettes or alcohol. Most recognize that this right would have to be linked to the idea that they are not harming others and that there would have to be some kind of regulation parallel to existing DUI laws and restricted smoking areas due to secondhand smoke. A key piece of information used in this debate is that marijuana has and continues to be the most commonly used illicit substance in America. In 1996, for instance, 32% of Americans in the household population (50% of those aged 25 to 34) had used marijuana in their lifetime, and 5% (6% of those aged 26 to 34) had used it in the past month (Office of Applied Studies [OAS], 1997a). By way of comparison, the lifetime and past-month rates of using all other illicit drugs (e.g., cocaine, crack, hallucinogens, inhalants, prescription drugs, and opioids) were only 18% and 3%, respectively. Moreover, the American public perceived the risk of marijuana use as lower than alcohol for both occasional use (44% vs. 54%) and regular use (60% vs. 77%). In addition, preliminary data from the 1997 National Household Survey on Drug Abuse (NHSDA; OAS, 1998) show that the perceived risk of using marijuana has dropped to a 10-year low. Thus, the argument is being made that there is a large minority that has and continues to use marijuana and should be allowed to do so as long as they are not harming others. Moreover, following in the wake of successful referenda allowing limited legalization of marijuana in California and Arizona, there will undoubtedly be more efforts in the 21 (mostly western) states that allow this

TABLE 4.1 Summary of Main Themes in the Marijuana Legalization Debate

	Common Proponent Arguments	Common Opponent Arguments
Right to Use	• Individuals should have the right to decide whether to use marijuana just like cigarettes or alcohol. • There is a large minority that has and continues to use marijuana and should be allowed to do so as long as they are not harming others.	• Most addictive substances are not legal because they hurt the individual and society—particularly adolescents.
Alternative Uses	• Marijuana may have important medicinal value and/or help relieve symptoms during chemotherapy. • Hemp can be grown for commercial use with such a low THC level as to have minimal illicit value. • Hemp could be a commercially viable alternative to tobacco for small farmers.	• Alternative and more effective drugs exist for the same purpose. • There are alternative fibers for the same purpose. • The commercial market for hemp is small. • Hemp might be diverted to the illegal product of marijuana.

Consequence of Use	• There are no or minimal consequences of marijuana use. • Many of the consequences that do exist are artifacts of the current laws (e.g., possession). • Marijuana use is not associated with property crime or violence and is thus more like alcohol and tobacco than like cocaine or heroin. • Dismiss claims of consequences as "myths" or propaganda.	• Increasing marijuana use is associated with increasing rates of dependence on marijuana, tobacco, alcohol, and other drugs, particularly among adolescents. • Increasing rates of marijuana use are associated with a wide range of other legal, social, emotional, and health problems. • Marijuana is a known carcinogen, can exacerbate or lead to lung conditions, and is associated with a range of other health problems.
Effectiveness of Regulations	• Current interdiction, incarceration, prevention, and treatment policies do not work. • Prohibition did not work.	• Current policies are not perfect, but they do work. • Prohibition was very effective.
Cost to Society	• Legalization would save enforcement, court, and prison costs. • Legalization could be used to generate another sin tax.	• Real costs to society would be in terms of increased rates of dependence and their associated psychological, family, and vocational problems. • Other legal costs from increased DUI (from alcohol and/or marijuana), and fights may consume savings. • Cost to adolescents is particularly high.

sizable minority to propose voter-initiated referenda. Although some
will fail, this ad hoc approach to legalization is likely to be a major
facet of the political landscape for the foreseeable future.

Opponents of legalization typically argue that most addictive
substances are not legal because they hurt the individual and society—
particularly adolescents. Moreover, marijuana is a gateway drug that
often leads to other drug use and problems (Johnson & Gerstein,
1998; Mustari, Markwood, Dennis, & Godley, 1997). The core of this
argument is that use is likely to harm the individual or others and
hinges largely on the remaining themes below.

Even though this issue can be informed by facts, the fundamental
issue is a question of how the rights of the individual and society can
be balanced. Clearly, tobacco and alcohol are both harmful substances
that we "chose" to keep/make legal in spite of the consequences.
Similarly, we have enacted and repeated numerous safety laws based
on what we as a society were willing to tolerate (e.g., 55 mph speed
limits, mandatory seat belt laws, and vagrancy laws). Thus we recognize that this is a "value" decision that society must make and that
a large minority would like the right to do so. But unlike 60 years ago,
this time we need to make a more informed and rational decision.
This we try to do below.

Alternative Uses

Medical Use

Many of the current ballot initiatives focus less on the overall
legalization of marijuana than on the legalization of its use in the
treatment of people with severe and/or terminal illnesses. Numerous
anecdotal reports have been given suggesting that marijuana may be
useful in treating nausea and/or stimulating appetite in those undergoing chemotherapy, with glaucoma, or being treated for AIDS. This
movement has recently gained significant momentum from meta-
analyses showing that the application of marijuana's active ingredient (delta-9-tetrahydrocannabinol, or THC) does appear to be useful
in treating the nausea associated with cancer chemotherapy and in
stimulating appetite (Voth & Schwartz, 1997).

The argument against the medical use historically has been
founded on three principals. First, other drugs that do the same things

are available. Second, marijuana is purported to be a carcinogen or at least a harmful substance. Third, there has been a lack of empirical studies evaluating marijuana use. While the latter increasingly is being addressed, it is important to note that these studies have produced very mixed results. The Voth and Schwartz (1987) article cited in favor of using pure THC also noted that they did *not* find evidence that the crude form of THC found in marijuana was sufficient to help with side effects and that both pure THC and crude marijuana acted like carcinogenic substances. Moreover, reports that marijuana might also be effective in relieving the side effects of HIV/AIDS treatments and improving appetite have not always held up under more rigorous preliminary examination (Whitfield, Bechtel, & Starich, 1997).

We believe that there is sufficient anecdotal and scientific evidence to support further research on the effectiveness of marijuana in the treatment of seriously and terminally ill patients. However, evidence on marijuana's effectiveness and safety is very mixed, and problems have been reported. In particular, marijuana may cause a variety of respiratory problems, and there is some evidence that it either is a carcinogenic substance or has similar negative consequences. While this is true of other medications for terminally or severely ill patients (e.g., azidothymidine or AZT), there are scores of examples where a rush to put substances into the marketplace led to significant negative consequences (e.g., amphetamine diet pills and thalidomide). The medical uses of marijuana and/or pure THC should be evaluated but with the full set of safeguards expected of any new product (although probably under the fast-track regulation given the severity of the conditions in question).

Commercial Use

The second alternative use that is often proposed is the legalization of hemp—a generic name for marijuana plants including those with such low THC levels as to have minimal illicit value. Hemp was one of the first plants cultivated by humans and has been used to make fabric and paper for over 10,000 years. It was grown by Presidents Washington and Jefferson, was a royally and then federally mandated crop during the 17th and 18th centuries, and was a federally subsidized crop in the United States as recently as World

War II. The U.S. government, however, has not issued a permit for growing hemp in 40 years (http://thehia.org/public/hempfacts.html).

Proponents of reissuing permits or deregulating commercial hemp use (summarized here from Roulac, 1997, and http://thehia.org/public/hempfacts.html) "assert" that hemp has many uses and one of the highest crop values per acre. Hemp seeds are one of the highest sources of essential fatty acids, complete protein (more of the digestible form than soy beans), and B-vitamins and contain 35% dietary fiber. Its bark produces one of the longest natural soft fibers that is longer, stronger and more absorbent than cotton fiber and also provides better insulation than cotton. It is important to note that, while almost half of the agricultural chemicals used in the United States are applied to cotton, hemp is asserted to grow well without herbicides, fungicides, or pesticides. If true, hemp would be a more sustainable and less polluting source of fiber for paper, be more resistant to yellowing and decomposition, and able to be recycled more often. Because of its high value per acre and many uses, hemp could be one of the few products that small family tobacco farmers switch to (in fact many switched to tobacco because hemp was removed from the market). The list of facts about hemp goes on and on like the ad for the hemp industry that it is.

While relatively small, commercial hemp production is on the rise and many countries have lifted previous bans in the past 5 years. Countries where commercial production is under way or being established are Australia, Austria, Canada, Chile, China, Denmark, Egypt, Finland, France, Germany, Great Britain, Hungary, India, Japan, The Netherlands, Poland, Portugal, Romania, Russia, Slovenia, Spain, Switzerland, Thailand, and the Ukraine (http://thehia.org/public/hempfacts.html). A major reason why production bans are being lifted is because hemp is a cash crop with one of the highest dollar value yields in agriculture: $750 to $1,250 per acre for the fiber and another $300 to $487 for the seeds (Oxford Hemp Exchange, 1998). It may also play an important role in efforts by the Robert Wood Johnson Foundation and several southeastern states to find alternative cash crops for small struggling family-owned tobacco farms (Reaves & Purcell, 1996). These families may be locked into tobacco farming because few other crops can pay the average $3,600 per acre gross of tobacco. Although this gross yield is much higher, the planting costs for tobacco are about $2,000 per acre and 5 to 10 times higher than those for hemp.

The arguments against commercialization tend to focus on two issues. The first is that the world hemp market has been relatively small for the past 20 years. Some have argued that the high cost per acre might actually work to keep down the demand even if hemp were commercialized (Bennett, McDougal, & Roques, 1995). Although the Hemp Taxation Act of 1933 did put an end to the industry, production of hemp had already fallen off to less than 200 acres in the whole United States in the preceding 5 years because it could not compete with other less expensive crops (e.g., cotton, flax, pulpwood) and/or cheap imports from overseas. When the Japanese overran the Philippines early in World War II, the U.S. military did have 146,000 acres planted (primary for marine rope), but this production died out after the war when hemp was replaced by stronger and less expensive nylon cord. Countries like Mexico that tried to keep their small hemp farmers going actually had to subsidize it (like the United States does with tobacco farms) because it was not commercially competitive with other products and/or hemp was produced less expensively in some African or South American countries.

A second issue is that marijuana (with a high THC content) could potentially be grown under the guise of being hemp because the plants are almost indistinguishable to the naked eye. This point is not in dispute by anyone, and it is relatively clear that the ulterior motive of many people wishing to reintroduce commercial hemp is, indeed, to either get a foot in the door of full legalization and/or provide cover for growing hemp that contains a meaningful level of THC. Opponents maintain that commercialization of hemp is unnecessary because of the available alternatives and that commercialization has enormous potential to create legitimacy and/or new sources of marijuana at a time when marijuana use is already on the rise.

Like the medication debate, many of the claims about the commercial value of hemp are just that—claims. If even partially true, hemp could indeed prove to be a valuable commodity. We have significant concerns about its true commercial viability and feel these claims may be grossly overstated. With increased production, the cost of hemp will come down unless there is an increase in demand. It is unclear from where these new markets would come without significant public or private commitments to research and development, and even with these commitments, it is still unclear if costs could be brought down sufficiently to make the products commercially viable alternatives to well-established natural and synthetic alternatives. In terms of public funds, policy-makers need to weigh some of the potential advantages (e.g., a replacement crop for small tobacco farmers, a less polluting crop) against the certainty that at least some of the hemp would be diverted into plants with a higher THC level for marijuana use. We believe that agricultural researchers and companies should be allowed to further explore the properties and commercial value of hemp, but that this development needs to be monitored and any commercial production taxed at a sufficient rate to cover the costs of a testing and monitoring program to assure that plants would be produced with THC content so low as to make them unsuitable for diversion into the illicit drug market.

Consequence of Use

Proponents of legalization often explicitly state (or imply) that (a) there are no or minimal consequences of moderate marijuana use, (b) the problems are no worse than those related to alcohol use, (c) many of the consequences that do exist are artifacts of the current laws (e.g., possession), and (d) marijuana is not a "hard drug" like cocaine or heroin because it is not associated with property crime, dependence, or health or emotional consequences. Proponents rarely offer more than anecdotal evidence and/or circular claims to support their positions; rather, they often try to argue against "myths" or propaganda put out by the "opponents" and/or the government (e.g., Zimmer & Morgan, 1997; http://www.visi.com/grp/infocanv/myths.html).

Opponents have argued that there is an extensive litany of evils that result from marijuana use (e.g., homicidal tendencies and giving males breasts) and that it is a gateway to heavier drug use. Although they are quick to give lists of problems they assert are caused by marijuana, they also primarily rely on anecdotal evidence or circular claims and focus on disproving the "myths" and propaganda of the opponents (vs. proving their own point).

Unfortunately, both sides often do a poor job of proving their own points or fairly weighing the evidence and instead simply cite their position in an ideological mantra. Complicating matters further, there is clear evidence the government did originally misrepresent the evidence it had against marijuana (Bonnie & Whitebread, 1970) and has repeatedly exaggerated problems (e.g., reefer madness, marijuana will make you murder, marijuana will clog up your arteries, marijuana will give you breasts). In a day and age when marijuana use is common, such exaggerated claims are only useful for a short time before they back fire. Now the government's (and many research) statements are routinely dismissed by the proponents even when they are well grounded, and, conversely, some government officials seem very reluctant to critically question the basis of the opponents' assertions.

So what do we know? Since most people would consider it unethical to randomly assign people to smoke marijuana, much of the evidence concerning its consequences is correlational. This said, there is substantial correlational evidence from large representative samples of an extensive array of negative consequences that vary proportionately with the frequency of use. For instance, among people (adults and adolescents) who have used marijuana in the past year, 40% reported one or more symptoms of dependence (indicating a need for treatment) in the National Household Survey on Drug Use (NHSDA; OAS, 1995a). Among those who used marijuana 12 or more times in a year, 60% reported one or more of these symptoms. These rates are very comparable to those associated with 12 or more days during the past year of using cocaine (26% and 62%) and alcohol (22% and 68%)—though lower than those associated with tobacco (59% and 76%) (OAS, 1997b). Moreover, Table 4.2 uses data from the NHSDA to show that the relationship between age of onset and having one or more symptoms of dependence as an adult varies significantly by age. Relative to people who start using as adults, those who start using marijuana between the ages of 15 and 17 are twice as likely to report a symptom of dependence as an adult; those who start under the age of 15 are six times as likely to report one or more symptoms. Note that in both cases this is a significantly higher rate of risk among adolescents than has sparked recent debate about tobacco and alcohol use (also shown in Table 4.2) and are very large effects in the field of public health.

TABLE 4.2 Probability and Relative Risk of Having One or More
Substance Disorder Symptoms as an Adult Based on Age
of First Use

| | Age of First Use of Substance (of lifetime users)[a] | | | | | |
| | Under 15 | | 15-17 | | 18+ | |
Substance Used	1+Sx	Odds	1+Sx	Odds	1+Sx	Odds
Lifetime tobacco users (N = 10,887)	26%	2.00	20%	1.54	13%	1.00
Lifetime alcohol users (N = 12,795)	27%	3.92	15%	2.12	7%	1.00
Lifetime marijuana users (N = 5,847)	24%	5.71	9%	2.16	4%	1.00

SOURCE: Dennis, McGeary, French, and Hamilton (1998).
a. All are significant at $p < .05$.

There is also substantial evidence that marijuana use is highly correlated with a wide range of other problems. Using data from the NHSDA again, we found that 14 out of 15 adolescents who used marijuana also used alcohol. Those who used marijuana and alcohol weekly were much more likely than nonusers in the past year to have had problems related to committing a crime (69% vs. 17%), attention deficit/hyperactivity/conduct disorder (57% vs. 4%), being involved in a major fight (47% vs. 11%), shoplifting (41% vs. 4%), being admitted to an emergency room (33% vs. 17%), committing a theft (33% vs. 4%), selling drugs (31% vs. 0%), damaging property (31% vs. 3%), dropping out of school (25% vs. 6%), being arrested (23% vs. 1%), and/or being on probation (16% vs. 1%) (McGeary, Dennis, French, & Titus, 1998). This is very much like other hard drugs and goes well beyond simple possession. Moreover, increases in problems are almost all directly proportional to the frequency of use—with low-frequency users having more problems than nonusers but fewer than high-frequency users. Finally, marijuana is also a respiratory irritant and delivers more tar to the lungs than cigarettes (Roth et al., 1998;

Van Hoozen & Cross, 1997; Voth & Schwartz, 1997; cf. Sidney, Quesenberry, Friedman, & Tekawa, 1997). Moreover, a study of marijuana's role as a potential carcinogen will need to study the synergistic impact of its combined use with alcohol and tobacco use (as is commonly done).

Several of the supposed "myths" about marijuana use have been addressed with empirical studies, including: (a) marijuana, tobacco and alcohol do appear to be one (of several) gateways to heavier drug use (Johnson & Gerstein, 1998; Mustari et al., 1997); (b) marijuana causes measurable physiological, cognitive, emotional and social impairment (Lundqvist, 1995; Millsaps, Azrina, & Mittenberg, 1994; Pope & Yurgelun-Todd, 1996; Roffman & Stephens, 1997; Solowij, 1995; Solowij, Grenyer, Chesher, & Lewis, 1995a; Solowij, Michie & Fox, 1995b), (c) THC is fat soluble, trapped in body fat/tissues and released slowly over time (Chiang & Hawks, 1986; Leighty, Fentiman & Foltz, 1976), and (d) marijuana use is now the most commonly mentioned substance among adolescents entering treatment, being seen in emergency rooms, and/or receiving autopsies (OAS, 1995a, 1995b, 1997a, 1997b). The presence of marijuana in so many autopsies needs to be explored further: Presumably it is contributing indirectly (e.g., DUI, fights, accidents) since overdosing on marijuana is virtually unheard of. Although there is no evidence yet of a specific toxic effect of accumulating THC in the body, it is associated with continuing physiological impairment that has been documented to persist up to 6 months after the last use among initially heavy users (Solowij, 1995; Solowij et al., 1995a, 1995b). While there are some mixed findings (endemic to observational research), most research to date suggests that more frequent and/or longer marijuana use is likely to lead to dependence and a wide host of major individual, family, and social problems. Proponents may still prefer to legalize marijuana, but they need to recognize that it is an addictive substance and that legalization is likely to lead to increased use and to exacerbate a wide range of problems. This is important because many proponents (e.g., Zimmer & Morgan, 1997; http://www.visi.com/grp/infocanv/myths.html) continue to cling to the belief that all of the problems are little more than propaganda—willingly dismissing correlational evidence much as smokers did throughout the 1960s and 1970s.

Effectiveness of Regulations

The proponents of legalization argue that the continued high use and acceptance of marijuana in spite of increased enforcement and penalties is prima facie evidence of the failure of current regulations. They frequently say that America's experiment with alcohol prohibition was an abject failure and cite data showing little or no change in the rates of alcohol use or problems in the years right before and after Prohibition "ended." These proponents also focus on claims that prohibition only serves to increase corruption (e.g., Carter, 1992; Nadelmann, 1991, 1992), and these points lead many to say or predict that the drug prohibition movement will prove to be a failure. They call either for outright deregulation or a shift back to state and local regulations that were more typical until about 60 years ago. Others note that prevalence data are predicted much less by changes in regulation than by changes in "perceived risk" (Harrison, Backenheimer & Inciardi, 1995).

Conversely, opponents of legalization argue that the continued high use and acceptance of marijuana is prima facie evidence of the need to redouble our prevention, treatment, and legal efforts to combat it. They argue that while people "chose" to repeal Prohibition, it was actually very effective and cite data from the years right before and after Prohibition was "introduced" to bolster their claims (Burnham, 1993; Moore, 1992a). They also acknowledge the role of "perceived risk" and/or "parental pressure" as a protective factor against use (e.g., Mustari et al., 1997).

Such counterclaims are among the most perplexing in this debate because both sides are nominally citing the same data. The incidence of marijuana use today is higher than any other illegal substance and rising back toward prior records from the late 1970s (and exceeding them for 8th graders) (Dennis & McGeary, in press; Institute for Social Research, 1998; OAS, 1998). The current high prevalence rates are like the proverbial glass of water filled to the middle—both half empty *and* half full. Whether this is cause for deregulation or tighter regulation goes back to the question of where to place the balance between individual freedom and consequences to society.

Regarding the interpretation of the historical effectiveness of prohibition, we believe the problem here is twofold. First, the proponents and opponents of regulations are looking at different periods of time. Second, we believe that both regulation and prevalence change in response to public opinion (i.e., their correlation is indirect or even spurious over short periods of time). Let's start by looking at alcohol consumption from 1710 to 1975 using per capita alcohol consumption data from Rorabaugh (1976, 1979). Alcohol use actually peaked at a mean annual consumption of 3.1 to 3.7 gallons per person between 1770 and 1830, fell off to 1.0 to 1.4 gallons between 1840 and 1900, and then rose again to 1.6 to 1.7 gallons in the 15 years leading up to Prohibition. During Prohibition the rates dropped off to 0.6 gallons per person, then went back to around 1.1 gallons after it was repealed, and rose gradually again to 2.0 in 1975. Thus, the initial passage of prohibition, which coincided with massive public displeasure with the rising rates of alcohol use (as evidenced by passing the prohibition amendment itself in two thirds of the states) did in fact precede a large decline in alcohol use. It also preceded major declines in the number of people seeking treatment for alcoholism and/or alcohol-induced medical disorders (Moore, 1992a, 1992b), as well as the demise of several major treatment organization and prevention movements (White, 1998). Conversely, in the period leading up to the repeal of prohibition, which coincided with increased public tolerance (as evidenced by the prohibition's repeal via an amendment), use and medical problems had slowly crept back up to their preprohibition rates and the laws were often going unenforced; consequently, there was little subsequent change when the actual amendment was nominally repealed. Thus, the problem is that both groups only look at part of the picture and ignore how regulations are only effective when they are reflections of public opinion and being enforced. Since regulation, enforcement, and prevalence typically change in response to public opinion, it is important to incorporate the latter into evaluations of regulations (e.g., looking back over longer periods of time, checking trends in public opinion, looking at the degree to which penalties or regulations are being enforced before they are "nominally" added or removed).

This three-way relationship between public opinion, legislation, and use can also be seen in reviews specific to marijuana (e.g., Harrison et al., 1995; Inciardi, 1991). The initial rise in marijuana use began in the 1950s and 1960s and peaked between 1969 and 1972. During the latter period, marijuana was nominally put on the same schedule of drugs as heroin and LSD (Controlled Substances Act of 1970), but at the same time, 42 states reduced penalties for marijuana possession and it was clearly part of the popular culture of the time. The second peak of use in the late 1970s followed a 5-year period during which 11 states decriminalized possession of small amounts of marijuana for personal use and the Carter administration was seriously discussing federal decriminalization of marijuana. This was followed by a barrage of anti-drug laws and prevention campaigns and decreasing use in the 1980s. Extending this analysis into the 1990s, we are currently experiencing 12-year record prevalence rates and record incidence rates among 8th graders (Institute for Social Research, 1998). Moreover, this coincides with a decade-long trend in which the general public is viewing marijuana as less and less harmful (OAS, 1998) and several states are again looking at decriminalizing some uses of marijuana.

Cost to Society

Proponents of legalization will typically argue that it would literally save the $3 billion to $10 billion currently spent on interdiction, enforcement, court, and prison costs and that legalization could be used to generate another sin tax that could serve to both regulate consumption and cover the additional costs of treatment (e.g., Friedman & Friedman, 1984; Nadelmann, 1991, 1992). Others focus on the role of drug prohibition in increasing violence, street crime, corruption, and generally supporting the underworld's illegal activity (e.g., Carter, 1992). Some also argue that the current widespread use of unregulated marijuana actually poses a health threat because there are effectively no limits on concentration, additives, or even the presence of pesticides. Finally, the cost to society of marijuana use is often compared with the much larger costs to society of alcohol and tobacco.

Opponents of legalization will generally concede that the cost of drug prohibition are great but argue that the costs of legalization are likely to be even greater (e.g., Bennet, 1992; Inciardi & McBride, 1991; Moore, 1992b; Wilson, 1992). They point out that during the period after the (re)legalization of alcohol in the United States and during the period of legalized heroin prescriptions in the United Kingdom, use of these substance did generally increase over a period of several years (note that analyses showing no effect are typically limited to short periods of time). Opponents say that like most products in the world the demand for marijuana is likely to be elastic and increase if the cost decreases. (Note that if the taxes on it were set so high to hold the price constant this would create a new black market and negate any gains from legalization.) Comparisons of the current cost to society of marijuana and alcohol are misleading since the former is currently illegal and the latter legal. This said, it is important to note that the estimated cost to society of alcohol abuse in 1990 was already several times higher than the criminal justice costs at $98.6 billion (Rice, 1993) and is now presumed to be even higher in 1998 dollars (National Advisory Council on Alcohol Abuse and Alcoholism Subcommittee on Health Services Research, 1998). Finally, the cost of adolescent alcohol use is particularly high as it comes at a critical time of development and is associated with a higher likelihood of ongoing problems as an adult (Dennis et al., 1998).

Some of the issues raised by proponents are legitimate as drug prohibition does cost billions of dollars each year, particularly as a result of state and federal drug laws that have resulted in record high drug-related arrests, court cases, and prison sentences (Inciardi, McBride, & Rivers, 1996). We can and probably should debate the relative merits of different allocations of these funds and look at their impact on the limited resources of our criminal justice system. However, there are several reasons why these costs would *not* simply go away as a result of legalization. First, there will be new regulatory costs to address the issues of quality and dosage as well as the likely prevention of underage use. Second, although many people are in drug court for charges related to marijuana use (31%), the next most common substance related to the charges is actually "misuse" (e.g., DUI, fighting) of alcohol (27%). Even if marijuana were legalized, it would probably still result in many criminal justices costs because (a) we are likely to pass laws holding people responsible for misusing it (e.g., DUI laws) and because of (b) the correlation between increasing marijuana use and increasing alcohol use, fighting, behavior problems and a variety of illegal activities discussed above. Compounding matters further, we believe that it is naive to think that full legalization of marijuana (or even just decriminalization) would not lead to increased use. Additionally, general assumptions that marijuana has few direct health consequences needs to be reevaluated in light of the correlation between increased use, lung problems, atten-tion problems, emergency room admissions, and treatment admis-sions. Although marijuana is not likely to result in an overdose, it is increasingly showing up in autopsies (particularly among adoles-cents) and is likely to be indirectly related to death (e.g., driving under the influence). Marijuana alone might not sufficiently impair driving, but its combined use with alcohol (exceeding 85% among adolescents) has a synergistic effect that does create major problems. Recent analyses of the NHSDA data show that those reporting one or more symptoms of marijuana dependence are less likely to be working and that those who are working work fewer hours (Bray, Zarkin, Dennis, & French, 1998). Thus, we believe that legalization may reduce some but not all criminal justice costs associated with marijuana use and that it is likely to dramatically increase other costs associated with health care and lost productivity.

Reprise, Implications, and Recommendations

In reviewing the marijuana legalization debate we have concluded that whether or not marijuana should be legal is fundamentally a "choice" that needs to be made between individual liberty and societal costs—and that this should be an "informed" choice. Although many Americans have some firsthand experience with marijuana, there is a significant amount of confusion about its use, consequences, and cost to society. Proponents and opponents of legalization make blan-ket statements that simply cannot both be true and in many cases even cite nominally the same data to support opposite conclusions. In our search for a middle ground we have tried to fairly review both sides and have concluded the following:

- There is sufficient anecdotal and scientific evidence to support further research on the effectiveness of marijuana in the treatment of seriously and terminally ill patients; however, we also believe that it is not a wonder drug or panacea, has significant potential to do harm, and should be evaluated within the framework of existing guidelines for new drugs.

- If the claims about hemp's agricultural properties prove to be true, it may be an important crop, but there are major unanswered questions about these properties and the crops' commercial viability relative to alternative crops and synthetic products; while we believe that agricultural researchers and businesses should be allowed to explore these issues, any commercialization program should include a user fee to cover the cost of a THC monitoring protocol to prevent the likely diversion problem it will create.

- There is substantial correlational evidence that the increasing rate of marijuana use is associated with increasing rates of marijuana dependence, other drug use, behavior problems, cognitive problems, health problems, and illegal activities (including those other than possession and dealing); moreover, these problems are significantly worse for adolescents than adults, so any discussion of legalization needs to address these issues and should continue exclusions for adolescent use.

- Regulations to control marijuana, alcohol, and other drug use have primarily been effective when they are reflections of public sentiment and enforced; looking over longer time periods and taking into account public sentiment and both federal and local regulation, we believe that regulations have reduced substance use but have not generally eliminated it.

- The current prohibition of marijuana is expensive, but legalization would *not* eliminate many of these costs and would increase other cost associated with misuse (e.g., DUI), substance abuse treatment, mental health treatment, health treatment, and result in a loss of workplace productivity; fundamentally we also believe legalization would increase demand and the number of active users.

Both sides make some valid points but also need to recognize some problems in their own argument and approach.

We believe that proponents will continue to argue for decriminalization and legalization of some or all uses of marijuana, but they need to recognize that it does indeed have negative consequences and will probably increase costs to society not reduce them. A serious effort in this vein needs to surpass libertarian issues and address practical questions about dose, quality, regulation, misuse legislation, and so forth (see other chapters in this volume). Proponents must also recognize that large numbers of people are already dependent on marijuana and need treatment. Unfortunately, there are no major self-help groups (e.g., AA, CA, NA) or treatment modalities that focus on marijuana use and little research on the effectiveness of current approaches for other drugs applied to this more general population (Roffman & Stephens, 1997).

Opponents of legalization must come to terms with the fact that many of their past claims have indeed been exaggerated. This might have worked in the 1930s when few people were familiar with marijuana, but today the material that was used then is now viewed as "satire" by a more educated public (e.g., the movie *Reefer Madness*). Opponents also need to move away from general statements (e.g., "just say no") or exaggerated claims and focus on the true consequences of marijuana use, much as is done with alcohol and tobacco. General prevention effort would also be wise to balance their efforts between relying solely on harder drugs (e.g., heroin, cocaine, crack) that are very problematic but rarely used and marijuana, which has less severe problems but is used by more than twice as many people as all the other illegal drugs combined.

According to the most recent national survey (OAS, 1998), by 1997 marijuana had been used one or more times by 33% of Americans over the age of 12 (about 71.1 million people) with significant variation by age: 12% of those aged 12 to 15, 33% of those aged 16 to 17, 41% of those aged 18 to 25, 48% of those aged 26 to 34, and 39% of those 35 or older. Moreover, about one out of seven of these lifetime marijuana users (about 11.1 million people) have used marijuana in the past month, with virtually all of these past month marijuana users also using alcohol and one third using other illegal drugs. In spite of the evidence reviewed above, people are increasingly viewing marijuana as less and less harmful. If they are to make an informed choice, the debate must move away from its current ideological basis and do a more fearless appraisal of the actual evidence.

Both sides also need to be careful to look separately at the issues related to adolescent use and even the consequences of their debate. This is the third major period in which our nation has debated criminalization and/or legalization; each period has been associated with increased use and decreasing ages of first use. Parental ambivalence about marijuana use (common among baby boomers who feel hypocritical since they were users) is statistically the equivalent of telling kids to "go for it." Unfortunately, the consequences and cost of adolescent initiation (particularly among those under age 15) is significantly higher than it was for their parents (who did not generally start using it until they were adults). Both policymakers and researchers also need to recognize the almost complete co-occurrence of alcohol use (and, to a lesser extent, tobacco use) among marijuana users. The effect of these two or three substances taken together may be very different from the effect of just one of them taken alone and needs to be studied.

◼ Conclusion

Robin Room (1978) has argued that social policies toward intractable problems—and the ownership of intractable problems that flow from these policies—are inherently unstable. That instability derives from an ever-changing status quo that everyone associated with the intractable problem finds unacceptable. This clearly describes the current debate over marijuana legalization. Marijuana is neither a wonder drug or the root of all evil. It is widely used, has some viable uses, has some negative consequences, and will have substantial costs to society whether marijuana is legalized or not. As we move toward a period of local variation in regulations, the single most important thing we need to do is adopt what the late Donald Campbell (1969) referred to as "an experimental approach to social reform." This means that although strategies for problem resolution may vary in response to rigorous evaluations that determine precisely which policies and programs do and do not ameliorate the problem, a commitment to the seriousness of a particular problem must be unwavering. We suggest that the exploration of any alterations in drug control policy be based on the following foundation.

- The strategy option must be explicitly and meticulously defined, with particular focus on both the goals to which the policy is directed and the means by which those goals will be achieved. Its consideration must be weighed not in the abstract but in the details.

- Establish credible baseline data regarding cannabis use and personal and social consequences of cannabis use prior to policy implementation that will make it possible to measure changes that accrue from various policies and policy enforcement variations.

- Prior to its implementation, identify and measure those variables that could influence (confound) the outcome of the policy experiment.

- Implement systems of evaluation prior to policy implementation. We need to clearly define "How will we know if this policy is or is not working? What measures will be used to evaluate the success or failure of the intervention?" Every effort should be made to protect data collection and evaluation from corruption by those whose personal or institutional interests are served or threatened by the policy.

As the dialogue regarding the need for any policy changes and the needed direction of those changes moves from narrow academic and policy circles to the mainstream citizenry (via referendum and increasing public attention), there is a growing need for more objective analysis of the facts. Although government and many community-based agencies have a major role to play in this process, they also need to recognize that their credibility has been compromised with many by putting out (or failing to discount) misleading or false information; they need to consider working with other arbitrators to facilitate a broader discussion (e.g., Robert Wood Johnson Foundation, 1998).

We believe that the general citizenry would be willing to tolerate legalization if it perceived marijuana as something that only had direct effects on an individual but would not be willing to tolerate it if it had direct effects on other individuals in terms of use (e.g., secondhand smoke) or misuse (e.g., DUI). Most people are willing to endorse medical or commercial research, and we recommend this as long as it is well designed and controlled. But the willingness to fully legalize marijuana is likely to be significantly hampered by the growing body of evidence that it does have consequences for the individual (e.g., dependence, cognitive impairment, dropping out of school, emergency room admissions, other drug use), consequences for others (e.g., behavior problems, fighting, theft), and that while some criminal justice costs might decrease, some will not and other costs to society are likely to rise (e.g., substance abuse treatment, health care, lost productivity). We, therefore, do not recommend that actual marijuana use be legalized until these issues are better understood and that active steps be taken to try to reverse the current tide of adolescent marijuana use. On the other hand, we do not believe that the punishment for using marijuana should be worse than its potential consequences. Historically, there have been periods when the hysteria over marijuana led to average jail terms for possession that were greater than for rape or murder (as they currently are for crack). Up until the 1960s, Texas still had laws on the books with terms of 2 years to life for marijuana possession (Bonnie & Whitebread, 1970).

This is out of proportion and not very constructive for the several million people already addicted to marijuana. There needs to be balance here as well.

■ References

Bennet, W. J. (1992). A response to Milton Friedman. In R. L. Evans & I. M. Berent (Eds.), *Drug legalization: For and against* (pp. 53-56). La Salle, IL: Open Court.

Bennett, S. S., McDougal, J., & Roques, W. (1995). *Hemp.* Elmhurst, IL: Drug Watch International.

Benjamin, D. & Miller, K. (1991). *Undoing drugs: Beyond legalization.* New York: Basic Books.

Bonnie, R. J., & Whitebread, C. H. (1970). The forbidden fruit and the tree of knowledge: An inquiry into the legal history of American marijuana prohibition. *Virginia Law Review, 56*(6), 971-1202.

Bray, J., Zarkin, G. A., Dennis, M. L., & French, M. T. (1998). *Symptoms of dependence, multiple substance use, and labor market outcomes.* Manuscript under review. Research Triangle Park, NC: Research Triangle Institute.

Burnham, J. (1993). *Bad habits: Drinking, smoking, taking drugs, gambling, sexual misbehavior and wearing in American history.* New York: University Press.

Campbell, D. T. (1969). Reforms as experiments. *American Psychologist, 24,* 409-429.

Carter, H. (1992). We're losing the drug war because prohibition never works. In R. L. Evans & I. M. Berent (Eds.), *Drug legalization: For and against* (pp. 91-94). La Salle, IL: Open Court.

Chiang, C. N., & Hawks, R. L. (1987). Implications of drug levels in body fluids: Basic concepts. In R. L. Hawks & C. N. Chiang (Eds.), *Urine testing for drug abuse* (NIDA Research Monograph 73, pp. 62-83). Rockville, MD: NIDA.

Dennis, M. L., & McGeary, K. A. (in press). Adolescent alcohol and marijuana treatment: Kids need it now. *TIE Communique.* Rockville, MD: Center for Substance Abuse Treatment.

Dennis, M. L., McGeary, K. A., French, M. T., & Hamilton, N. (1998). *The need for more adolescent treatment and treatment research.* Manuscript submitted for publication.

Friedman, M., & Friedman, R. (1984). *Tyranny of the status quo.* San Diego: Harcourt Brace Jovanovich.

Harrison, L. D., Backenheimer, M., & Inciardi, J. A. (1995). *Cannabis use in the United States: Implications for policy.* Available: http://www.frw.uva.nl/cedro/library/Drugs16/usa.html. Newark: University of Delaware, Center for Drug and Alcohol Studies.

Inciardi, J. A. (Ed.). (1991). *The drug legalization debate.* Newbury Park, CA: Sage.

Inciardi, J. A., & McBride, D. C. (1991). The case against legalization. In J. A. Inciardi (Ed.), *The drug legalization debate* (pp. 45-79). Newbury Park, CA: Sage.

Inciardi, J. A., McBride, D. C., & Rivers, J. E. (1996). *Drug control and the courts.* Thousand Oaks, CA: Sage.

Institute for Social Research. (1998). *Monitoring the Future study.* Ann Arbor: University of Michigan. Available: http:// www.isr.umich.edu/src/mtf

Johnson, R. A., & Gerstein, D. R. (1998). Initiation of use of alcohol, cigarettes, marijuana, cocaine, and other substances in US birth cohorts since 1919. *American Journal of Public Health, 88*(1), 2733.

Leighty, E. G., Fentiman, A. F., & Foltz, R. L. (1976). Long-retained metabolites of -9- and -8-tetrahydrocannabinol identified as novel fatty acid conjugates. *Research Communications in Chemical Pathology and Pharmacology, 14,* 13-28.

Lundqvist, T. (1995). Cannabis use in a drug and alcohol clinic population. *Drug & Alcohol Dependence, 39*(1), 29-32.

McGeary, K. A., Dennis, M. L., French, M. T., & Titus, J. C. (1998). *National estimates of marijuana and alcohol use among adolescents: Overlap in use and related consequences.* Manuscript submitted for publication.

Millsaps, C. L., Azrin, R. L., & Mittenberg, W. (1994). Neuropsychological effects of chronic cannabis use on the memory and intelligence of adolescents. *Journal of Child and Adolescent Substance Abuse, 3,* 47-55.

Moore, M. (1992a). Actually, prohibition was a success. In R. Evans & I. Berent (Eds.), *Drug legalization: For and against.* Lasalle, IL: Open Court.

Moore, M. (1992b). Drugs: Getting a fix on the problem and the solution,. In R. L. Evans & I. M. Berent (Eds.), *Drug legalization: For and against* (pp. 123-156). La Salle, IL: Open Court.

Mustari, E., Markwood, A., Dennis, M., & Godley, M. (1997). *Patterns of drug use and consequences among Illinois students.* Bloomington, IL: Lighthouse Institute.

Nadelmann, E. A. (1991). The case for legalization. In R. L. Evans & I. M. Berent (Eds.), *Drug legalization: For and against* (pp. 19-26). La Salle, IL: Open Court.

Nadelmann, E. A. (1992). The case for legalization. In J. A. Inciardi (Ed.), *The drug legalization debate* (pp. 17-44). Newbury Park, CA: Sage.

National Advisory Council on Alcohol Abuse and Alcoholism Subcommittee on Health Services Research. (1998). *Improving the delivery of alcohol treatment and prevention services. A national plan for alcohol health services research.* Rockville, MD: National Institute on Alcohol Abuse and Alcoholism.

Office of Applied Studies. (1995a). *Drug abuse warning network. Annual medical examiner data 1995* (Series D-1, prepared by CSR Inc.). Rockville, MD: Substance Abuse and Mental Health Services Administration.

Office of Applied Studies. (1995b). *National household survey on drug abuse.* Rockville, MD: Substance Abuse and Mental Health Services Administration.

Office of Applied Studies. (1997a). *Main findings from the 1996 National Household Survey on Drug Abuse.* Rockville, MD: Substance Abuse and Mental Health Services Administration.

Office of Applied Studies. (1997b). *National admissions to substance abuse treatment services. The treatment episode data set (TEDS) 1992-1995* (Advanced Report

No. 12, prepared by B. Ray, R. Thoreson, L. Henderson, & M. Toce). Rockville, MD: Substance Abuse and Mental Health Services Administration.

Office of Applied Studies. (1998). *Preliminary results from the 1997 National Household Survey on Drug Abuse.* Rockville, MD: Substance Abuse and Mental Health Services Administration.

Oxford Hemp Exchange. (1998). *Agronomic data.* Available: http://www.pbmo.net/oxhemp/commo.html

Pope, H. G., & Yurelun-Todd, D. (1996). The residual cognitive effects of heavy marijuana use in college students. *Journal of the American Medical Association, 275*(7), 521-527.

Reaves, D. W., & Purcell, W. (1996). *Beyond the controversy: What happens to the tobacco producers? Virginia's Rural Economic Analysis Program.* Available: http://www.reap.vt.edu/reap/isstob.htm

Rice, D. P. (1993). The economic cost of alcohol abuse and alcohol dependence: 1990. *Alcohol Health and Research World, 17*(1), 10-11.

Robert Wood Johnson Foundation. (1998). *Call for proposals: Substance abuse policy research program 1998, round IV.* Available: http://www.phs.wfubmc.edu/sshp/rwj/rwj.htm

Roffman, R. A., & Stephens, R. S. (1997). Assessment and treatment of cannabis dependence. In D. L. Dunner, (Ed.), *Current psychiatric therapy II* (pp. 147-153). Philadelphia: W. B. Saunders.

Room, R. (1978). *Governing images of alcohol and drug problems: The structure, sources and sequels of conceptualizations of intractable problems.* Unpublished doctoral dissertation, University of California, Berkeley.

Rorabaugh, W. J. (1976). Estimated U.S. alcoholic beverage consumption, 1790-1860. *Journal of Studies on Alcohol, 37,* 360-361.

Rorabaugh, W. J. (1979). *The alcoholic republic: An American tradition.* New York: Oxford University Press.

Roth, M. D., Arora, A., Barsky, S. H., Kleerup, E. C., Simmons, M., & Tashkin, D. P. (1998). Airway inflammation in young marijuana and tobacco smokers. *American Journal of Respiratory Critical Care Medicine, 157*(3, Pt. 1), 928937.

Roulac, J. (1997). *Hemp horizons : The comeback of the world's most promising plant.* White River Junction, VT: Chelsea Green.

Schwartz, R. H., Voth, E. A., & Sheridan, M. J. (1997). Marijuana to prevent nausea and vomiting in cancer patients: A survey of clinical oncologists. *Southern Medical Journal, 90*(2), 167-172.

Sidney S., Quesenberry, C. P., Friedman, G. D., & Tekawa, I. S. (1997). Marijuana use and cancer incidence. *Cancer Causes Control, 8*(5), 722-728.

Sloman, L. (1979). *Reefer madness: The history of marijuana in America.* New York: Bobbs-Merrill.

Solowij, N. (1995). Do cognitive impairments recover following cessation of cannabis use. *Life Sciences, 56*(23/24), 2119-2126.

Solowij, N., Grenyer, B., Chesher, G., & Lewis, J. (1995). Biopsychosocial changes associated with cessation of cannabis use: A single case study of acute and chronic cognitive effects, withdrawal and treatment. *Life Sciences, 56*(23/24), 2127-2134.

Solowij, N., Michie, P. T., & Fox, A. M. (1995). Differential impairments of selective attention due to frequency and duration of cannabis use. *Biological Psychiatry, 37,* 731-739.

Van Hoozen, B. E., & Cross, C. E. (1997). Marijuana: Respiratory tract effects. *Clinical Review of Allergy and Immunology, 15*(3), 243-269.

Voth, E. A., & Schwartz, R. H. (1997). Medicinal applications of delta-9-tetrahydro-cannabinol and marijuana. *Annals of Internal Medicine, 126*(10), 791-798.

White, W. L. (1998). *Slaying the dragon: A history of addiction and recovery in America.* Bloomington, IL: Lighthouse Institute.

Whitfield, R. M., Bechtel, L. M., & Starich, G. H. (1997). The impact of ethanol and marinol/marijuana usage on HIV+/AIDS patients undergoing azidothymidine, azidothymidine/dideoxycytidine, or dideoxyinosine therapy. *Alcohol Clinical and Experimental Research, 21*(1), 122-127.

Wilson, J. Q. (1992). Against the legalization of drugs. In R. L. Evans & I. M. Berent (Eds.), *Drug legalization: For and against* (pp. 27-46). La Salle, IL: Open Court.

Zimmer, L., & Morgan, J. P. (1997). *Marijuana myths, marijuana facts: A review of the scientific evidence.* New York: Lindesmith Center.

Cannabis, The Wonder Drug

LESTER GRINSPOON

In September 1928, Alexander Fleming returned from vacation to his laboratory and discovered that one of the petri dishes he had inadvertently left out over the summer was overgrown with staphylococci except for the area surrounding a mold colony. That mold contained a substance he later named penicillin. He published his finding in 1929, but the discovery was ignored by the medical establishment, and bacterial infections continued to be a leading cause of death. More than 10 years later, under wartime pressure to develop antibiotic substances to supplement sulfonamide, Howard Florey and Ernst Chain initiated the first clinical trial of penicillin (with 6 patients) and began the systematic investigations that might have been conducted a decade earlier (Hayes et al., 1993).

After its debut in 1941, penicillin rapidly earned a reputation as "the wonder drug of the 1940s." There were three major reasons for that reputation: (1) It was remarkably nontoxic, even at high doses; (2) it was inexpensive to produce on a large scale; and (3) it was extremely versatile, acting against the microorganisms that caused a great variety of diseases, from pneumonia to syphilis. In all three respects, cannabis suggests parallels:

1. *Cannabis is remarkably safe.* Although not harmless, it is surely less toxic than most of the conventional medicines it could replace if it were legally available. Despite its use by millions of people over thousands of years, cannabis has never caused a death. The most serious concern is lung damage from smoking, but that can easily be addressed by increasing the potency of cannabis and by developing the technology to separate the particulate matter in marijuana smoke from the cannabinoids (prohibition, incidentally, has prevented this technology from flourishing). Once cannabis regains the place in the U.S. Pharmacopoeia that it lost in 1941 after the passage of the Marijuana Tax Act (in 1937), it will be among the least toxic substances in that compendium.

2. *Medical cannabis would be extremely inexpensive.* Street marihuana today costs $200 to $400 an ounce, but the prohibition tariff accounts for most of that. A reasonable estimate of the cost of cannabis as a medicine is $10 to $20 an ounce, or about 25 cents per marijuana cigarette. As an example of what this means in practice, consider the following. Both the marijuana cigarette and an 8 mg ondansetron pill (cost: $20) are effective in most cases for the nausea and vomiting of cancer chemotherapy (although many patients find cannabis to be more useful). Thus cannabis would be nearly 100 times less expensive than the best present treatment for this symptom.

3. *Cannabis is remarkably versatile.* The following is a brief review of some of the symptoms and syndromes for which it is useful.

Pain

There are many anecdotal reports of marijuana smokers using the drug to reduce pain: postsurgery pain, headache, migraine, menstrual cramps, and so on. In particular, marijuana is becoming increasingly recognized as a drug of choice for pain that accompanies muscle spasm. This kind of pain is often chronic and debilitating, especially in paraplegics, quadriplegics, other victims of traumatic nerve injury, and people suffering from multiple sclerosis or cerebral palsy. Many of these sufferers have discovered that cannabis not only allows them to avoid the risks of opioids for pain relief but also reduces muscle spasms and tremors, sometimes allowing them to leave their wheelchairs (Petro, 1980). Cannabis may act by mechanisms different from those of other analgesics. Some new synthetic cannabinoids might prove to be especially effective as an analgesic—a possibility implied by the recent discovery of cannabinoid nerve receptor sites in the brain and other organs (Matsuda et al., 1990; Munro et al., 1993).

Seizures

About 20% of epileptic patients do not get much relief from conventional anticonvulsant medications. Cannabis has been explored as an alternative at least since a case was reported in which marijuana smoking together with the standard anticonvulsants, phenobarbital and diphenylhydantoin, enabled the control of seizures in a young epileptic man (Consroe et al., 1975). The cannabis derivative that is most promising as an anticonvulsant is cannabidiol. In one controlled study, cannabidiol in addition to prescribed anticonvulsants produced improvement in 7 patients with grand mal (whole body) convulsions; 3 showed great improvement. Of 8 patients who received a placebo instead, only 1 improved (Cunha et al., 1980). Again, the evidence is anecdotal, yet there are patients suffering from both grand mal and partial seizure disorders who find that smoking marijuana allows them to lower the doses of conventional anticonvulsant medications or dispense with them altogether (Grinspoon & Bakalar, 1993).

Asthma

Asthma is a breathing disorder that arises when bronchial muscles go into spasm and the pathway to the lungs is blocked by mucus and swelling. A number of antiasthmatic drugs are available, but they all have drawbacks—limited effectiveness or side effects. Because marijuana dilates the bronchi and reverses bronchial spasm, cannabis derivatives have been tested as antiasthmatic drugs. Smoking marijuana would probably not be a good way to treat asthma because of chronic irritation of the bronchial tract by tars and other substances in marijuana smoke, so recent researchers have sought a better means of administration. THC in the form of an aerosol spray has been investigated extensively (Tashkin et al., 1975, 1977). Other cannabinoids such as cannabinol and cannabidiol may be preferable to THC for this purpose. An interesting finding for future research is that cannabinoids may affect the bronchi by a mechanism different from that of the familiar antiasthmatic drugs.

Glaucoma

Cannabis may also be useful in the treatment of glaucoma, the second leading cause of blindness in the United States. In this disease, fluid pressure within the eyeball increases until it damages the optic nerve. About 1 million Americans suffer from the form of glaucoma (open angle) treatable with cannabis. Marijuana causes a dose-related, clinically significant drop in intraocular pressure that lasts several hours in both normal subjects and those with the abnormally high ocular tension produced by glaucoma. Oral or intravenous THC has the same effect, which seems to be specific to cannabis derivatives rather than simply a result of sedation. Cannabis does not cure the disease, but it can retard the progressive loss of sight when conventional medication fails and surgery is too dangerous (Hepler et al., 1976).

It remains to be seen whether topical use of THC or a synthetic cannabinoid in the form of eyedrops will be preferable to smoking marijuana for this purpose. So far, THC eyedrops have not proved effective, and in 1981 the National Eye Institute announced that it would no longer approve human research using these eyedrops (Roffman, 1982). Other natural cannabinoids and certain synthetic cannabis derivatives are still being studied. But smoking marijuana (6 to 10 times a day) seems to be a better way of titrating the dose than taking an oral cannabinoid, and most patients apparently prefer it.

Cancer Treatment

Cannabis derivatives have several minor or speculative uses in the treatment of cancer and one major use. As appetite stimulants, marijuana and THC may help to slow weight loss in cancer patients (Regelson et al., 1976). THC has also retarded the growth of tumor cells in some animal studies, but results are inconclusive. Another cannabis derivative, cannabidiol, seems to increase tumor growth (White et al., 1976). Possibly, cannabinoids in combination with other drugs will turn out to have some use in preventing tumor growth.

But the most promising use of cannabis in cancer treatment is the prevention of nausea and vomiting in patients undergoing chemotherapy. About half of patients treated with anticancer drugs suffer from severe nausea and vomiting, and for 30% to 40% of them, the commonly used antiemetics do not work (Roffman, 1982, pp. 82-83). The nausea and vomiting are not only unpleasant but a threat to the effectiveness of the therapy. Retching can cause tears of the esophagus and rib fractures, prevent adequate nutrition, and lead to fluid loss. Some patients find the nausea so intolerable they say they would rather die than go on.

The antiemetics most commonly used in chemotherapy are phenothiazines, such as prochlorperzine (Compazine) and the relatively new ondansetron (Zofran). The suggestion that cannabis might be useful arose in the early 1970s when some young patients receiving cancer chemotherapy found that marijuana smoking, which was of course illegal, reduced their nausea and vomiting. In one study of 56 patients who received no relief from standard antiemetic agents, 78% became symptom free when they smoked marijuana (Vinciguerra et al., 1988). Oral THC has proved effective where the standard drugs were not (Lucas & Laszlo, 1980; Sallan et al., 1975). But smoking generates faster and more predictable results in both glaucoma and cancer treatment because it raises THC concentration in the blood more easily to the needed level (Chang et al., 1979). Also, it may be hard for a nauseated patient to take oral medicine. In fact, there is strong evidence that most patients suffering from nausea and vomiting prefer smoked marijuana to oral THC (Grinspoon & Bakalar, 1993).

Oncologists may be ahead of other physicians in recognizing the therapeutic potential of cannabis. In the spring of 1900, two investigators randomly selected more than 2,000 members of the American Society of Clinical Oncology (one third of the membership) and mailed them an anonymous questionnaire to learn their views on the use of cannabis in cancer chemotherapy. Almost half of the recipients responded. Although the investigators acknowledge that this group was self-selected and that there might be a response bias, their results provide a rough estimate of the views of specialists on the use of dronabinol (Marinol) and smoked marijuana.

Only 43% said the available legal antiemetic drugs (including oral synthetic THC) provided adequate relief to all or most of their patients, and only 46% said the side effects of these drugs were rarely a serious problem. Of this study, 44% had recommended the illegal use of marijuana to at least one patient, and half would prescribe it to some patients if it were legal. On average, they considered smoked marijuana more effective than oral synthetic THC and roughly as safe (Doblin & Kleiman, 1991).

AIDS

The American AIDS epidemic first came to notice in 1981, and by now more than 150,000 Americans have died of the disease. Nearly 2 million are infected with the HIV virus, and perhaps as many as a quarter-million are ill. Although the spread of AIDS has slowed among homosexuals, the reservoir is so huge that the number of cases is sure to grow. Women and children as well as both heterosexual and homosexual men are now being affected; the disease is spreading most rapidly among inner-city Black and Hispanic intravenous drug abusers and their sexual partners. The period of incubation (between infection and the development of symptoms) is variable, but averages 8 to 10 years. It appears that almost all infected persons will eventually become ill. No cure is known. Opportunistic infections and neoplasms (cancerous growths) can be treated in standard ways, and the virus itself can be attacked with antiviral drugs, of which the best known is zidovudine (AZT). Unfortunately, AZT along with other drugs used in the treatment of AIDS sometimes causes severe nausea that heightens the danger of semistarvation for patients who are already suffering from nausea and weight loss because of the illness.

Marijuana is particularly useful for patients who suffer from AIDS because it not only relieves the nausea but retards weight loss by enhancing appetite. When it helps patients regain lost weight, it can prolong life. The synthetic cannabinoid dronabinol (Marinol) has been shown to relieve nausea and retard or reverse weight loss in patients with HIV infection, but most patients prefer smoked cannabis for the same reasons that cancer chemotherapy patients prefer it;

it is more effective, has fewer unpleasant side effects, and the dosage is easier to adjust.

Depression

Cannabis was first proposed as a treatment for depression by Jacques de Tours in 1845 (de Tours, 1857). During the next 100 years his proposal was supported and disputed in a number of medical papers. The most recent study on cannabis and depression was undertaken in 1973. Eight hospitalized patients were given either THC or a placebo for up to a week. The THC did not help them, and in 4 it produced discomfort and anxiety so serious it had to be withdrawn (Kotin et al., 1973). But the patients were not prepared for the experience of an altered state of consciousness, and the brief duration of the trial must also be considered. Standard anti-depressants often require 3 weeks or longer to work. Today, among the minority of depressed patients who do not respond to any of the standard antidepressants or find the side effects unbearable, some have discovered that whole smoked marijuana is more useful than any legal drug (Grinspoon & Bakalar, 1993). This evidence is anecdotal, and large-scale clinical studies will eventually be required.

Marijuana has more in common with penicillin than safety, low cost, and medical versatility. There are also historical parallels. Just as World War II provided the impetus for research on penicillin as an antibiotic, the AIDS epidemic is now exerting some pressure on researchers to explore cannabis as a medicine. But it took more than 10 years to recognize the medical potential of penicillin, and its systematic exploration was long delayed by lack of interest and resources. For similar reasons, the urgently needed large double-blind clinical studies on cannabis have not yet begun. In this case, progress has been delayed largely because the medical establishment and government authorities are stubbornly committed to wild exaggeration of marijuana's dangers when it is used for nonmedical purposes. In fact, the potential dangers of marijuana when taken for pleasure and its usefulness as a medicine are historically and practically interrelated issues: historically, because the arguments used to justify public and official disapproval of recreational use have had a strong influence on opinions about its medical potential; practically, because the more evidence accumulates that marijuana is relatively safe even when used as an intoxicant, the clearer it becomes that the medical requirement of safety is satisfied.

If any other drug had shown similar promise, public and professional interest would be intense. But the U.S. government, in its zeal to prosecute the "War on Drugs," has been doing everything it can to reduce that interest and prevent the fulfillment of marijuana's medical promise (Grinspoon et al., 1995). Cocaine and morphine (Schedule II drugs) are legally available as medicines; marijuana is not. In 1972, an effort began to put marijuana in Schedule II, a classification that would allow doctors to prescribe it. Finally, in 1988, after years of hearings in which scores of witnesses presented impressive evidence of marijuana's medical usefulness, an administrative law judge recommended that it should be transferred to Schedule II. The Drug Enforcement Administration rejected the recommendation and was upheld on appeal.

It is distressing to consider how many lives might have been saved if penicillin had been developed as a medicine immediately after Fleming's discovery. It is equally frustrating to consider how much suffering might have been avoided if cannabis had been available as a medicine for the past 55 years. Initial enthusiasm for drugs is often disappointed after further investigation. But it is not as though cannabis were an entirely new agent with unknown properties. Studies conducted in the past 10 years have confirmed a centuries-old promise. I believe that as restrictions on research are relaxed and this promise is realized, cannabis will come to be recognized as a wonder drug of the 1990s.

◼ References

Chang, A. E., et al. (1979). Delta-9-tetrahydrocannabinol as an antiemetic in cancer patients receiving high-dose methotrexate: A prospective, randomized evaluation. *Annals of Internal Medicine, 91,* 819-824.

Consroe, P. F., .et al. (1975). Anticonvulsant nature of marihuana smoking. *Journal of the American Medical Association, 234,* 306-307.

Cunha, J. M., et al. (1980). Chronic administration of cannabidiol to healthy volunteers and epileptic patients. *Pharmacology, 21,* 175-185.

de Tours, J. J. M. (1857). Lypemanie avec stupeur; tendance a la demence—traitement par l'extrait (principe resineux) de cannabis indica—Guerison. *Lancette Gazette Hopital, 30*, 391.

Doblin, R., & Kleiman, M. (1991). Marihuana as anti-emetic medicine: A survey of oncologists' attitudes and experiences. *Journal of Clinical Oncology, 9*, 1275-1280.

Grinspoon, L., & Bakalar, J. B. (1993). *Marihuana, the forbidden medicine* (pp. 1-23). New Haven, CT: Yale University Press.

Grinspoon, L., Bakalar, J. B., & Doblin, R. (1995, September 7). Marijuana, the AIDS wasting syndrome, and the U.S. government. *New England Journal of Medicine, 333*(10), Letters to the Editor, 670-671.

Hayes, G. W., et al. (1993). The golden anniversary of the silver bullet. *Journal of the American Medical Association, 270*(13), 1610-1611.

Hepler, R. S., et al. (1976). Ocular effects of marihuana smoking. In M. C. Braude & S. Szara (Eds.), *Pharmacology of marihuana.* New York: Raven Press.

Kotin, J., et al. (1973). Delta-9-tetrahydrocannabinol in depressed patients. *Archives of General Psychiatry, 23*, 345-348.

Lucas, V. S., & Laszlo, J. (1980). Delta-tetrahydrocannabinol for refractory vomiting induced by cancer chemotherapy. *Journal of the American Medical Association, 243*, 1241-1243.

Matsuda, L. A., et al. (1990). Structure of a cannabinoid receptor and functional expression of the cloned DNA. *Nature, 346*, 561-564.

Munro, S., et al. (1993). Molecular characterization of a peripheral receptor for cannabinoids. *Nature, 365*, 61-65.

Petro, D. J. (1980). Marihuana as a therapeutic agent for muscle spasm or spasticity. *Psychosomatics, 21*, 81-85.

Regelson, W., et al. (1976). Delta-9-tetrahydrocannabinol as an effective anti-depressant and appetite stimulating agent in advanced cancer patients. In M. C. Braude & S. Szara (Eds.), *Pharmacology of marihuana* (pp. 763-776). New York: Raven Press.

Roffman, R. A. (1982). Marihuana as medicine. *Madrona, 99.*

Sallan, S. E., et al. (1975). Antiemetic effect of delta-9-tetrahydrocannabinol in patients receiving cancer chemotherapy. *New England Journal of Medicine, 293*, 795-797.

Tashkin, D. P., et al. (1975). Effects of smoked marihuana in experimentally induced asthma. *American Review of Respiratory Diseases, 112*, 377-386.

Tashkin, D. P., et al. (1977). Bronchial effects of aerosolized delta-9-tetrahydro-cannabinol in healthy and asthmatic subjects. *American Review of Respiratory Diseases, 115*, 57-65.

Vinciguerra, V., et al. (1988). Inhalation marihuana as an antiemetic for cancer chemotherapy. *New York State Journal of Medicine, 88*, 525-527.

White, A. C., et al. (1976). Effects of delta-9-tetrahydrocannabinol in Lewis lung adenocarcinoma cells in tissue culture. *Journal of the National Cancer Institute, 56*, 655-658.

Thinking About the Drug Policy Debate

ERICH GOODE

ost participants in the drug policy debate are either hawks or doves; that is, they argue in favor of criminalization and against legalization of the currently illegal drugs or in favor of legalization and against criminalization. Proponents of both sides of the debate tend to ignore four fundamental fallacies to which all skeptical observers must pay close attention. These four fallacies ignore crucial distinctions—distinctions that make a difference in the validity of a given argument: (1) ignoring the very basis of the debate, that is, whether it is <u>consequentialist or moralistic</u>; (2) ignoring the distinction between absolute and relative deterrence; (3) ignoring unanticipated consequences; and (4) ignoring the middle ground between the hawks' and the doves' positions. I argue here that this middle ground is *harm reduction* and that it constitutes the sanest, most reasonable, and empirically grounded of all drug policy positions.

▓ A Brief History of Drugs and Policy

The history of American drug policy is marked by a series of fateful events. The passage of the Harrison Narcotic Act in 1914 certainly belongs in that company. Originally framed as a revenue measure, a series of Supreme Court decisions between 1919 and 1923 interpreted the Act as criminalizing the possession and sale of cocaine and narcotics. Another fateful event was the passage of the Marihuana Tax Act in 1937. Although, again (this time, deviously) couched in the impersonal language of revenue collection, this Act was designed to stamp out the use of what was then referred to as "the weed of madness."

In recent memory, perhaps no event stands out as more monotonous than Ronald Reagan's series of speeches in the 1980s launching what he dubbed the "War on Drugs" (in the footsteps of Lyndon Johnson's "War on Poverty"). The metaphor has captured the fancy of observers of the drug scene; it has become the central image guiding our view of the issue, challenging us to stand on one or the other side of a virtual Continental Divide. What's your stand on the War on Drugs? Are you *for* it or *against* it? Borrowing from Vietnam-era terminology, policy analyst Peter Reuter (1992) dubs the supporters of this "war" *hawks* and its opponents *doves*.

The hawks are the defenders of the War on Drugs; they support drug criminalization, drug prohibition and feel that a *punitive* policy toward the possession and sale of the currently illegal drugs is a good idea. To solve the drug problem, they say, we need to *punish* the user, the dealer, the supplier, the smuggler, and the manufacturer. Arrest them, they argue, ignore legal niceties, technicalities, and loopholes, and put them away for long prison sentences. Taking it even a step further, the most extreme hawkish position is held by observers who believe that the penalties for drug possession and sale should be increased. These include, for example, William Bennett, former federal drug "czar," who has been quoted as saying that anyone who sells an illegal substance to a minor *should be beheaded* (Lazare, 1990, p. 25), or Darryl Gates, former Los Angeles police chief, who stated that "marijuana smokers should be taken out and shot because we're in a war" (Beers, 1991, p. 38). The hawkish side of the debate figures that the way to deal with the problem of drug abuse is to wage something resembling an outright war; they further assume that this war *can* be won, *and*, to fight that war, we can rely mainly on criminal or penal sanctions—imprisonment, incarceration, a good, stiff prison sentence for drug violators. The only problem with drug criminalization, the most emphatic of them argue, is that we simply don't lock up enough drug users and sellers for a sufficiently long prison sentence. If we did, they say, this war could be won.

On the other side of this imaginary Continental Divide, we find the doves, the opponents of criminalization, drug prohibition, and penal sanctions for drug use and sale. The doves believe we should lay down our weaponry and declare a truce. We should deal with or attempt to solve the drug problem in an entirely different way, they argue—humanely, that is, medically and therapeutically. Devise a system whereby drugs will be placed in the hands of persons who cannot live without them. By devising such a system, the legalizers insist, the price of illegal drugs will decline, organized crime will collapse, dealers will stop killing one another, users and addicts will stop killing themselves, and society will not have to pay for the high cost of law enforcement (Nadelmann, 1988, 1989, 1992, 1995; Trebach, 1993). An even more extreme position along the criminalization-decriminalization axis is that advocated by the radical free market libertarians—Thomas Szasz and Milton Friedman (Friedman & Szasz, 1992; Szasz, 1992) being the two most vocal and prominent proponents—who argue that we should completely decriminalize the currently illicit drugs and remove all criminal penalties on the possession and sale of all psychoactive substances. Essentially, they argue, we should allow any and all adults to do anything they wish with these substances; the state should get out of the drug control and dispensation business altogether.

There is a great deal of self-righteousness on both sides of the Continental Divide. All too many of its combatants paint their own position as blatantly and self-evidently true. Once I have revealed the truth, they seem to argue, only villains and fools will disagree with me. For whatever evil or self-interested motives, my opponents refuse to see the facts and acknowledge what is staring them in the face, they insinuate; at the very least, incompetent, at worst, they are treacherous, stupid, biased. Read or listen to *my* argument, they seem to be saying, and you will be convinced. If you are not, well, there's something terribly wrong with you.

My intent here is to splash some cold water on such righteousness, set aside oracular and prophetic pronouncements, and introduce a more inquisitive, skeptical, Socratic, and empirical stance into the argument. In place of the view that truth can emerge only by bludgeoning one's opponents into oblivion, I expose some fallacies that apply equally to both sides of the debate. Many—possibly most—of the positions argued in the drug legalization-criminalization debate are based on fallacies and misconceptions. On either side, the policy they suggest cannot work because the world simply does not work that way. These policies cannot work because they fail to take into consideration certain crucial facts or dimensions or because they ignore certain basic distinctions. Many of these proposals have blind spots. They are based on erroneous and idealistic assumptions about human nature (or, at the very least, the American version thereof). I must reiterate that holding such misconceptions is not a monopoly of only one side of this debate—either the prohibitionist or "hawkish" side or the legalization or "dovish" side. Almost all parties to this debate, it seems, fall victim to one or another fallacious line of reasoning.

■ Fallacy 1:
Ignoring the Basis of the Drug Policy Debate

Our first fallacy is ignoring the very fundamental and crucial distinction between consequentialist, empirical, or utilitarian arguments, on the one hand, and arguments that are at bottom symbolic, idealistic, ideological, and moral, on the other. This means that in this debate we have the proponents of four entirely different arguments: consequentialist-legalizers, consequentialist-prohibitionists, idealistic-legalizers, and idealistic-prohibitionists.

Consequentialist-legalizers will argue that the drug laws are bad specifically because of the manifestly and measurably harmful consequences they have because they produce results that can both be readily measured and that can be widely agreed upon as harmful. On the other side of the debate, *consequentialist-prohibitionists* say that legalizing the currently illicit drugs will result in more harm, not less. Does criminalization or legalization result in a greater body count? In more disease? In a greater total cost to society? In a total concrete package that we all, more or less, can agree is better or worse? These are the sorts of questions the consequentialists ask, whether for or against punitive policies, whether for or against drug legalization.

The problem is that most observers and combatants are *not* consequentialists. Most are moralists or idealists. Moralists argue from a very different position from that of consequentialists; they are concerned about issues of justice and injustice. *Idealist-legalizers'* position is that the drug laws are bad because they are, by their very nature, unjust and unfair. On the other side, the drug laws are good, because it is right and proper to make a condemnatory statement about drugs. It's wrong, moralists who are also legalizers will say, to penalize one category of drug user and leave another untouched. It's immoral, they say, to force arrest and imprisonment on persons who victimize no one but themselves. It's bad, they argue, to force addicts to choose between imprisonment and treatment when it would be so much more enlightened to allow them to reach the decision to seek treatment on their own. On the other side, again, moralists who are also prohibitionists say, oh no, it's entirely appropriate to criminalize marijuana and leave alcohol legally tolerated because marijuana is much more of a corrupting drug than alcohol. James Q. Wilson, adopting this position (1990), argues that alcohol and cigarettes *shorten* human life, whereas cocaine and heroin *debase* it.

The distinction is lost on me, but the point should be clear: The moral argument is quite beyond the reach of empirical evidence. It pretends to be empirical, quite rational and reasonable, but it is not really based on consequentialist logic. The *moralist-legalization* position says that, regardless of what the law's practical or empirical consequences are, society has no right to pass or enforce laws against nonvictim behavior. Such laws are by their very nature unjust and immoral and hence do not deserve to exist. On the other side, *moralist-prohibitionists* say that society has no right to sanction or tolerate immoral behavior. The fact is, the logic on both sides is the same. The only difference is just *what* is designated immoral.

Consequentialists respond to the moralists' argument with a dismissive "So what?" It is a non sequitur they say, to argue, for example, that one drug is criminalized while another, even more harmful one, is legally tolerated. There are many reasons for each drug's legal status, only one of which is the harm a given substance can cause. In response to the argument that a drug should be outlawed because its use is immoral, consequentialists respond by asking, what do you *mean* "immoral"? Who decides? For consequentialists, the question of justice simply does not enter into the equation. Sure, societies have a right to protect themselves against all manner of victimizing behavior. Everybody agrees on that. But is it unjust to criminalize *nonvictim* behavior? Or, to paraphrase the title of Peter McWilliams's (1993) book, is it "nobody's business" if you do? Are laws against consensual acts—acts between consenting adults—as McWilliams asserts, inherently absurd? The consequentialists say, this is a meaningless argument. Who says it isn't society's business to protect its citizens from harm? According to what criteria? What if a given law results in a lower body count? Less disease, less physical harm and, I might add, less criminal victimization? A better total concrete package? If it does, then who *cares* what the moralists say. Yes, the consequentialists say, a society does have the right to keep citizens from harming themselves—if our criteria include less concrete harm. Are the seat belt and the helmet laws too repressive? Too bad! They save lives, say the consequentialists. Without them, the rest of us would have to pick up the pieces in the form of shattered bodies and hospital bills (Goldstein & Kalant, 1990).

The question of whether they work, in the sense that they actually do reduce the undesired behavior, is a completely separate issue, the consequentialists say. All too often, moralists have wrapped one argument up into the other. That is, the *moralist-legalizer*s want it both ways: They say, people ignore the laws and do what they want anyway. But they also say that the laws are too restrictive and repressive. Well, which is it? Consequentialists argue that all civilized societies have a responsibility to protect persons who take risks with their own lives, risks that exceed a certain statistical likelihood of occurring. And, to consequentialists, that's the end of the of argument.

In a nutshell, to the consequentialist, the basis of the moralist's argument is irrelevant. To the moralist, the basis of the consequentialist's argument is flawed. In assessing arguments on both sides of the Continental Divide, one would do well to pay close attention to whether a proponent of a given position is a consequentialist or a moralist.

◼ Fallacy 2:
Ignoring Absolute Versus Relative Deterrence

The second fallacy also characterizes the thinking of both the prohibition and the legalization sides of the debate. Both commit the same fallacy; both reify the "War on Drugs"; both mistake a metaphor for a concrete reality. On the prohibition side, the error is imagining that the drug war is winnable; on the legalization side, it is imagining that not winning the drug war indicates a catastrophic failure of drug prohibition. More generally, the fallacy is the inability to distinguish between *absolute* deterrence and *relative* deterrence. Absolute deterrence makes use of a "hard" or "strict" punitive or prohibitionist argument. It says that an activity can be eliminated—or at the very least drastically reduced—by law enforcement. Escalate the arrest and imprisonment of the number of addicts and users, and use will decline precipitously; as a consequence, illegal drug use will be "defeated." This was Reagan's and Bush's take on the drug war. In this sense, then, the "War on Drugs" has truly been a failure. As the legalizers say, drug abuse is still with us and in abundance.

The second kind of deterrence, relative deterrence (or the "soft" or "moderate" punitive position), argues that in the absence of any punishment whatsoever rates of a given activity would be higher. Saying that rates of drug use are high and therefore the drug laws are a failure makes no more sense to the relative deterrence argument than saying that law enforcement has not eliminated rape, robbery, murder, and theft; and therefore we ought to legalize these currently criminal activities. Ethan Nadelmann, perhaps the most well-known of the legalizers, makes a great deal of what he cleverly refers to as the "push-down/pop-up" principle (1988, p. 9). The reason why law enforcement cannot wipe out drugs at their source, Nadelmann says, is that every time you push down production and distribution in one location, it "pops up" somewhere else. Drugs are so hugely profitable to sell that, when the illicit activities of a given dealer, distributor, or even area or country are closed down, one or more

daring enterprising entrepreneurs will always step in, take the necessary risks, and distribute the product whose flow was temporarily
interrupted. Moreover, the riskier the operation, the higher the potential profit—and the more daring and enterprising the dealers who
come out of the woodwork.

Nadelmann is right or at least half right. He is right in the sense
that push-down/pop-up does take place. Experience shows that, taken
as a whole, drug distribution cannot be stamped out. Part of the
reason is prohibition itself; outlawing a very desirable substance
increases its cost and hence its profitability. But he is wrong in the
sense that stamping out drug distribution must be our only measure
of the effectiveness of law enforcement. It is naive to take the absolute
deterrence argument at face value. What would drug use be like in
the absence of law enforcement is an even more compelling issue, I
would argue. Thus, not only are the "War on Drugs" people wrong in
assuming that drug use can be stamped out, the legalization people
are wrong in assuming that absolute deterrence is the only form of
deterrence.

Relative deterrence reasoning is far more modest in its aims. It
says that criminalization need not eliminate or even drastically
reduce drug use. All it needs to do is *contain* it. Keep it within certain
boundaries. The soft or moderate criminalization position says that
stamping out drug use is a futile and literally impossible task—and
here, Reagan and Bush were clearly wrong. At the same time, stamping out drug use is an absurd measure of the effectiveness of the drug
laws. Legalizers who argue that "everyone knows" that the drug laws
have failed are basing their argument solely on the hard or strict
punitive approach. It leaves the soft or moderate criminalization
argument completely untouched. Would rates of use rise in the
absence of the drug laws? It would take an overly optimistic person
to believe otherwise. John Kaplan, legal scholar and staunch critic of
the drug laws and their enforcement, has said that the legalization
argument totally ignores some of the most basic laws of pharmacology
(1988, p. 33). Certainly, drug use would rise, and significantly so,
under almost any conceivable form of legalization.

Most people would not use the currently illicit drugs, and here
the "worst case scenarists" such as William Bennett who argue that
tens of millions of currently nonusing Americans would become
cocaine addicts, are completely wrong. No, the people whose use

would rise the most are not the current nonusers but the heaviest *current* users. They are the ones who do not use as much as they would like. Every time drug researchers interview them, users complain that it is too much of a "hassle" to use as much as they would really like. If it were less of a hassle to get their drugs of choice, they would use a lot more. Think of what a paradise legalization would be for them, they would get their drug supply from both barrels—legal and illegal sources. Under legalization, their use would double or triple. And they would die in much greater numbers than they do today.

Kaplan's position, which argues that relative deterrence does work, in no way contradicts his recognition that absolute deterrence does not work. Confusing these two forms of deterrence has rendered most arguments on both sides of the Continental Divide pretty much meaningless. It is clear that the warfare metaphor sets the prohibitionists up for inevitable failure and makes their argument fatally vulnerable to criticism.

When encountering an argument either for or against the current punitive policy or for or against some form of legalization, it is wise to keep the distinction between absolute and relative deterrence in mind.

◼ Fallacy 3:
Ignoring Unanticipated Consequences

A third fallacy is the failure to consider what sociologists refer to as *unanticipated consequences*. Legal scholars Franklin Zimring and Gordon Hawkins (1992) refer to the failure to take unanticipated consequences into consideration as the "trickle down fallacy" (pp. 109-110). A critic designs a program to reform what is wrong with the system, and from then on everything proceeds without a hitch—on paper, anyway. In real life, things are likely to be quite different. In contrast, as the great Scottish poet Robert Burns reminds us (put into modern English): "The best-laid schemes of mice and men often go awry." All too many participants in both the pro- and the antilegalization camps seem to have a grand, naive, and childish faith that there is a simple, one-to-one correspondence between their plan and its intended outcome—between motive and result. All that is necessary for our plan to work, they seem to imply, is a robust critique of the opposition and a motive that is pure of heart. The criminalization side says this: Imprison drug offenders, and drug offenses will decline and we will all be better off. The legalizers say this: Remove all criminal penalties on currently controlled substances, and drug dealers will stop killing one another, junkies will stop dying in such large numbers and we will all be better off. Do not worry about the details, both sides seem to say, what counts is the big picture. Set up our plan, and everything will fall into place. Everything we plan for will trickle down into all particulars of the program and in all locales. One legalization advocate, Arnold Trebach (1993) adopts this "let the chips fall where they may" approach. Let us legalize first, he says, and worry about the details later on. Drug prohibition is so bad, such a position argues, that legalization could not possibly be worse. Many proponents of legalization regard demands for the precise details of their plan as misleading prevarication.

I submit that advocates of the trickle-down position simply lack imagination. They fail to picture all the truly horrible things, those currently unanticipated things that could and, I submit, will, happen. As an anonymous wag once put it, remarking on Murphy's Law, "Murphy was a raving optimist." In the history of the world, for every policy that's ever been put in place, the trickle-down approach does not work, has not worked, and cannot work. Things all too often happen that are not planned. Outcomes take place that were not anticipated. Moreover, as anyone in the policy sciences will tell you, serendipity, or "happy accidents," are a lot less common than the unplanned-for catastrophes. Does anyone want to go back and reread what the early supporters of the Russian revolution had to say about putting the socialist agenda in place?

Two not-so-minor examples in the drug arena illustrate my point. In the 1970s and 1980s, the United States government backed the Afghan rebels in their fight against the Soviet invasion. This helped finance a terrorist organization that was involved in illegal opium production and dedicated to the destruction of the United States. State Department officials call this a "blowback." Sociologists refer to it as unanticipated consequences. In the 1980s, U.S. and Peruvian officials cooperated to eradicate opium production from the highlands of Peru. This resulted in assisting another terrorist organization,

Sendero Luminoso, which was aimed at bringing down the Peruvian state and fomenting a worldwide revolution. It seems that our anti-drug efforts created something of a power vacuum in the region into which *Sendero* stepped. Not only do the most sincere efforts often produce results that were not anticipated, they may also produce results that are very much undesired by observers of almost every stripe. Surely there's a lesson in these examples. The more we look at drug policy, the larger that unanticipated consequences loom and the more fallacious trickle-down thinking becomes. To quote the 20th-century architect Ludwig Mies van der Rohe, "God is in the details." I would add, "And so is the devil, and so is humankind."

Once again, every time an argument supporting one or another drug policy position is run by you, think about the "many a slip between the cup and the lip," or that intentions mean little in the face of unanticipated consequences.

▪ Fallacy 4: Ignoring the Middle Ground

Peter Reuter (1992), one of our eminently sane drug policy analysts, divides the drug policy debate into three camps—not just the two that are on either side of this artificial Continental Divide. As we saw, two of them are the hawks and the doves. But there is a third category: the "owls." Our most fervid debaters tend to ignore this middle ground, pretending that anyone who opposes their wise and sane proposals gives aim and comfort to the enemy. (To his credit, Nadelmann does not adopt this either-or thinking.) Reuter does not exactly equate the owls with the consequentialists who wish to reform the drug laws, but permit me to take liberties with his labels (because I am so very fond of them). Allow me to refer to the owls as pragmatists, utilitarians, strict cost-benefit analyzers—in a simple phrase, *harm reductionists*. I see myself as an owl. I reject the extremes on both sides of the debate; that is, I am neither a hawk nor a dove. I have come to the position in my thinking about the question of drug legalization that the pragmatic, utilitarian, or consequentialist position says a lot more about dealing with the drug problem than either the outright legalization position or the position that drug prohibition alone is the answer. The more I look at the drug problem, the less idealistic and the more pragmatic I become. The harm reduction program is an eclectic, mixed-bag set of proposals. Harm reduction is uninterested in the issue of ideology or morality. Essentially, just about the only standard by which a plan is evaluated is harm to the society, including the body count. What program reduces the body count? What program reduces death and disease? What program reduces victimization behavior? (Monetary costs clearly enter into this equation as well.) Find out what program does these things and adopt it.

If, under a certain plan, there is a risk that more people use drugs but fewer die, then again it is the body count that decides. Does that mean trying to control the legal drugs, alcohol and tobacco—for instance, through higher taxes or totally eliminating vending machines? Then let's do it; let's try to reduce their use since that would result in a lower body count. If that means keeping hundreds of thousands of heroin addicts on maintenance doses, so be it. If that means criminalizing one drug and legalizing another—and abandoning a generalist or "one size fits all" orientation toward all psychoactive substances—that's fine. If it means recognizing that drug use can never be wiped out—that, in the words of Mark Kleiman (1988), we have to "quit dreaming of a drug-free America" (p. E21)—let's do it. As with violent behavior such as robbery and rape, totally or substantially eliminating illicit drug use is simply beyond the capacity of the criminal justice system. We have to be satisfied with much more modest goals. If our harm reduction strategy means forcing addicts into treatment programs with the threat of imprisonment, it is all to the good. Expand drug maintenance, especially methadone programs. Expand drug education programs; and devise an educational program that works, for clearly and demonstrably, D.A.R.E. does not (Clayton, Cattarello, & Johnstone, 1996). Expand needle exchange programs (Des Jarlais et al., 1996). Expand condom distribution programs. Experiment with or study the feasibility of heroin maintenance programs. Seriously study programs of legal control in other locales, such as Amsterdam, Liverpool, and Switzerland. Set up criteria to determine whether or not they work. Go to these locales and talk to law enforcement agents, treatment personnel, policy analysts, and members of the general public. If there are features of these programs that look good and could be adapted to the American setting, then adopt them. If there are none, then look elsewhere. Be flexible and pragmatic: think about the many ways that might reduce harm from drug abuse. If one aspect of the program fails, scuttle it and try something else. Be experimental, be experiential, be empirical. Remember that *drugs are not the enemy*, harm to society and its members is the enemy. Whatever reduces the volume of harm is all to the good.

No one who supports harm reduction policies questions the fact that there are theoretical, political, and practical difficulties and dilemmas in implementing such a program. Here are at least three such problems: (1) Determining and weighing exactly what constitutes harm in the first place is an almost insoluble task; (2) how do we choose one or another total package of outcomes, each with its own mixture of good and bad? and (3) it is a political rather than an ideological matter. In an era of "lock 'em up and throw away the key," what politicians (indeed, what segments of the general public) support our owlish "harm reduction" strategies? Very few.

In spite of practical impediments to a rational, sane drug policy, there are two strong points in favor of programs of harm reduction. One is appeals to moral suasion. If we can get others to accept the evidence (which is itself a Herculean task), then who can question the moral weight of saving lives? This invocation relies on a fundamental principle that is widely accepted. The sanctity of human life, though often violated, remains a rhetorical "ace in the hole" for the harm reductionists. And second, unlike programs based on legalization—or, for that matter, those based on criminalization as a matter of principle—harm reduction programs can be adopted piecemeal, pragmatically, one step at a time, one feature at a time, one locale or jurisdiction at a time.

I am not so naive that I believe that in the head of someone, somewhere, who reads what owls have to say, a light is going to turn on and he or she will exclaim, "Aha! That's it!" and run out and immediately implement some version of the harm reductionist plan. A lot of political and ideological assumptions will have to be laid on the table and examined, hashed out, and resolved. However, the fact is, policy changes in controversial areas do take place over time. And if enough debate and discussion is stirred up, and enough observers, commentators, and critics begin to think along "harm reduction" lines, it is possible that some aspects of this program will be adopted here or there sometime in the 21st century. At that point, perhaps, instead of focusing on idealistic, ideological, moralistic, and symbolic issues, we can begin saving lives.

■ References

Beers, D. (1991, July/August). Just say whoa! *Mother Jones*, pp. 52-56.

Clayton, R. R., Cattarello, A. M., & Johnstone, B. M. (1996). The effectiveness of drug abuse resistance education (project D.A.R.E.): 5-year follow-up results. *Preventive Medicine, 25*, 307-318.

Des Jarlais, D. C., et al. (1996). HIV incidence among injecting drug users in New York City syringe-exchange programmes. *Lancet, 348*, 987-991.

Friedman, M., & Szasz, T. (1992). *On liberty and drugs: Essays on prohibition and the free market*. Washington, DC: Drug Policy Foundation Press.

Goldstein, A., & Kalant, H. (1990). Drug policy: Striking the right balance. *Science, 249*, 1513-1521.

Kaplan, J. (1988). Taking drugs seriously. *Public Interest, 98*, 32-50.

Kleiman, M. A. R. (1988, October 16). Quit dreaming of a drug-free America. *New York Times*, p. E21.

Lazare, D. (1990, January 23). The drug war is killing us. *Village Voice*, pp. 22-29.

McWilliams, P. (1993). Nobody's business if you do: The absurdity of consensual crimes in a free society. Los Angeles: Prelude Press.

Nadelmann, E. A. (1988). The case for legalization. *Public Interest, 92*, 3-31.

Nadelmann, E. A. (1989). Drug prohibition in the United States: Costs, consequences, and alternatives. *Science, 245*, 939-947.

Nadelmann, E. A. (1992). Thinking seriously about alternatives to drug prohibition. *Daedalus, 121*, 85-132.

Nadelmann, E. A. (1995, January 26). Europe's drug prescription. *Rolling Stone*, pp. 38-39.

Reuter, P. (1992). Hawks ascendant: The punitive trend of American drug policy. *Daedalus, 121*, 15-52.

Szasz, T. (1992). *Our right to drugs: The case for a free market*. New York: Praeger.

Trebach, A. S. (1993). For legalization of drugs. In A. S. Trebach, & J. A. Inciardi (Eds.), *Legalize it! Debating American drug policy*. Washington, DC: American University Press.

Wilson, J. Q. (1990, February). Against the legalization of drugs. *Commentary*, pp. 21-28.

Zimring, F. E., & Hawkins, G. (1992). *The search for a rational drug policy*. Cambridge, UK: Cambridge University Press.

Why the Drug War
Will Never End

STEVEN JONAS

The drug war is a primarily violent effort ostensibly aimed at the use by a minority of the already small number of users of an arbitrarily determined subset of the recreational mood-altering drugs. It does wreak havoc on certain sectors of non-White neighborhoods and imprisons relatively large numbers of mostly young non-White males. However it has had no, and by its "supply-side" nature could not have had, a demonstrable effect on illicit drug use.

AUTHOR'S NOTE: This chapter is based in part on a paper delivered at the Tenth International Conference on Drug Policy Reform, held in Washington, D.C., on November 9, 1996. I wish to acknowledge and thank Mark Mauer of the Sentencing Project (Washington, D.C.) for his help over the years in providing me with essential data on imprisonment for drug-related offenses.

Nevertheless, there are five reasons why the drug war will never end. First, it has a racist basis: Although about 75% of regular illicit drug users are White, since the war is waged almost entirely in non-White neighborhoods about 75% of those imprisoned for drug-related offenses are non-White. Thus it is highly useful politically. Second, defenders of the drug war at the same time often hold two contradictory views of drug use overall, a state of mind known as "cognitive dissonance." Among other things, this makes it impossible for them to develop a rational, effective national policy for dealing with *all* drug use, of which alcohol and tobacco are by far the most harmful to the nation's health and social fabric.

Third is the use by drug war defenders of "data-free policy making." Fourth is the interest of the major drug dealers, the tobacco and alcohol industries, in maintaining the drug war just as it is. Fifth is the fundamental weakness of the libertarian-dominated "drug policy reform movement." With the presence of these five factors in the field, one must conclude that the drug war and its attendant horrors for those upon whom it is waged will never end.

The Drug War and Its Targets

The "drug war" is no more about drugs than rape is about sex (thus the quotation marks around the term). Both rape and the drug war are about violence and control. The primary tools of the drug war range from the forcible attempts to stop Latin American peasants from growing the coca plant, to the domestic employment of some-times physically violent but in any case often unannounced and therefore mentally violent searches and seizures that in many other circumstances would be held to be unconstitutional, to the imprisonment of certain illicit drug users for nothing more than simple possession of the banned substance.

Ostensibly these methods are employed for the purpose of effecting a change in human behavior related to the regular use by a relatively small number of persons of an arbitrarily determined subset of the recreational mood-altering drugs (RMADs). The principal RMADs in terms of numbers of users and health/social harms caused by them are nicotine in tobacco and ethyl alcohol (Institute for Health Policy [IHP], 1993). The subjects of the drug war are certain of the much less used so-called *illicits*—primarily marijuana, heroin, and cocaine.

In 1996, in the month prior to being surveyed on the subject, 13 million (6.1%) of the population aged 12 and older used an illicit drug (Substance Abuse and Mental Health Services Administration [SAMHSA], 1997). Of these 13 million, 10 million were marijuana, not *hard drug*, users. The definition of "illicit" includes prescription psychoactive drugs such as tranquilizers and barbiturates when used on a nonprescription basis. These numbers are small when compared with the counts of regular tobacco and alcohol users, 69 million and 109 million, respectively. But whether the numbers of users of the illicits are relatively large or relatively small, the true goals of the drug war, unstated though they may be, are not concerned with the use of illicit drugs. In fact they could not be.

The Drug War and the Supply Side

First, the drug war focuses almost entirely on the supply side of the drug-use equation (Bloom, 1997; National Drug Control Strategy, 1997, chap. 1), trying to reduce/eliminate the use of its target RMADs by reducing/eliminating their retail supply. It uses this strategy and continues to do so even though over quite some time its efforts have been shown to have little impact upon either illicit drug supply or price (MacCoun & Reuter, 1997). Second, even if the drug war did have an impact on the supply of the substances with which it is concerned, the historical evidence is clear that for any of the RMADs (unless physically completely eliminated from the marketplace) simple availability has little impact on level of use (Jonas, 1997, p. 780).

For example, in the United States since 1965 in the face of unlimited and cheap drug supply (and expensive nationwide promotion, to boot), the proportion of adults who are cigarette smokers has dropped by about 40%. Following the end of Prohibition, it took 30 to 40 years before per capita consumption of ethyl alcohol in beer had reached its pre-Volstead Act level (Lender & Martin, 1982). Again this was in the face of unlimited, cheap supply (and expensive nationwide promotion, to boot).

Take the case of cocaine supply itself. As the federal government's own National Drug Control Strategy (NDCS, 1997, p. 21) tells us, the drug war, aimed primarily at supply over time, has had no measurable impact on cocaine availability. According to the NDCS, it did not vary between 1985 and 1995. That is to say, there was always more than enough of the drug available to meet any existing demand. Yet, again according to the NDCS (1997, p. 10), the number of regular users of cocaine declined from 5.7 million (3.0% of the population aged 12 and older) in 1985 to 1.5 million (0.7% of the population) in 1995. If simple availability were the key stimulus to use, a decline of that magnitude could not possibly have taken place.

There are two points here. First, the drug war, emphasizing as it does supply control and waged vigorously during this time, has simply not achieved its objective of reducing supply. Nor could it achieve its objective physically. Its targets are "small volume" drugs,[1] and history has shown that prohibition is effective only against large-volume drugs. Thus by its very nature the drug war could not possibly have much effect on illicit drug-use rates. Second, even if it could be effective in reducing the street availability of, say, cocaine, if the societal objective is reducing illicit drug use, *it is simply not necessary* to wage the drug war, for as we have seen, between 1985 and 1995 cocaine usage dropped by 280% (330% on a *per capita* basis) despite the drug war's inability to achieve its primary objective of controlling simple availability. Yet the war continues, both unabated and ineffective (Duke, 1995; Shannon, 1990).

Effective Anti-Drug Use Interventions

The ineffective drug war drags on, despite the fact that by employing nonviolent, public health-based interventions the United States has somewhat effectively dealt with much more widely used and much more broadly harmful RMAD carriers such as tobacco. As noted, that success has been achieved in the context of very strong efforts by the drug merchants to *promote* the use of their products on a nationwide basis through the media, virtually without limitation (a phenomenon that in the illicit drug market occurs only on a very limited, highly localized scale).

The True Agenda of the Drug War

This evidence is all central to revealing the true agenda of the drug war. That agenda is sharply highlighted by the following data. Drug war violence is aimed at the use only of an arbitrarily determined subset of the RMADs whose use is minor when compared to that of alcohol and tobacco. That subset happens to have a *use-related* negative health impact on the U.S. population that can be considered relatively minor when compared with the major negative health impacts of the use of alcohol and tobacco.

To be sure, the illicits are responsible for 20,000 to 40,000 deaths per year (McGinniss & Foege, 1993; NDCS, 1997, p. iv), about one half of which result from the drug war itself, not drug use (Goldstein, Brownstein, Ryan, & Bellucci, 1990; Greenberg, 1990). That is a substantial number—1% to 2% of all deaths. But alcohol and tobacco use are responsible for about 530,000 deaths per year—over *one quarter* of all U.S. deaths (McGinniss & Foege, 1993).

Furthermore, as noted, the drug war is aimed primarily at an arbitrarily determined minority subset of the already relatively small group of users of those drugs (Mauer & Huling, 1995). That further subset, approximately 22% of all illicit drug users (SAMHSA, 1995, p. 12) is defined primarily by skin color and ethnicity. The vast White majority of illicit drug users (75% of the total) are little affected by the drug war unless they happen to be particularly unlucky or foolhardy. Hence, the drug war and its implementation are filled with contradictions.

The Drug War and Decriminalization of the Anti-Drug Laws

Consider that in the broader context of the anti-drug laws in general it happens that to one extent or another *all* of the RMADs are illegal. Yet for *most* people, *most* of the laws covering most of the drugs are decriminalized.

For example, it is illegal to sell tobacco and alcohol to underage persons. So too is it illegal to sell prescription psychoactive drugs on a nonprescription basis to anyone. However, just as the laws banning the sale and even possession of the illicits are enforced with relative infrequency against White persons and in White neighborhoods, so too are the laws against the sale of tobacco and alcohol products to underage people and prescription psychoactives on a nonprescription basis to anyone rarely enforced on anyone.

It should be noted that in 1996 there were over 55% more regular users of prescription psychoactive drugs on a nonprescription basis than there were regular users of heroin and cocaine put together (SAMHSA, 1997). But virtually no middle- or upper-class White female is in prison for possession of illegally obtained Valium or Phenobarbital.

It should also be noted that the physical efforts of the drug war domestically to reduce the available supply of illicit drugs happen to be focused almost entirely on non-White neighborhoods. This is so even though, given the widespread residential racial segregation that characterizes the United States, the majority of illicit drug use must take place in White neighborhoods.

None of these facts have any relevance for a truly committed defender of the drug war (known colloquially as "drug warrior"), however, such as New York City's Mayor Rudolph Giuliani, former Senator Bob Dole, *New York Times* columnist A. M. Rosenthal, Dr. Herbert Kleber, and policy analyst Joseph Califano have demonstrated on repeated occasions (Califano, 1993; Cooper, 1997; Kleber, Califano, & Demers, 1997; Nagourney, 1996; Rosenthal, 1990, 1993, 1996; Shea, 1997).

Five Reasons Why the Drug War Will Never End

The first reason why the drug war will never end is its racist nature, which should by now be apparent. It is well known that major racist enterprises in the United States such as residential segregation, job discrimination, and inequality in educational opportunity serve certain major political, economic, social, and corporate ends. The drug war is a useful adjunct for this enterprise.

The second reason is what can be termed the "cognitive dissonance" that afflicts most observers, policy analysts, and policymakers who concern themselves with the drug problem. That is, they hold two entirely contradictory policy positions at the same time, and they will defend each to the death (of many drug users). Therefore, it becomes intellectually impossible to develop a rational national policy for effectively dealing with the many health and social problems caused by and/or associated with the use of RMADs.

Almost all of these contradictions stem from the fact that most drug policy analysts in the United States see two separate drug problems: those caused by the use of tobacco and alcohol (the incorrectly named "legal" drugs) and those caused by the use of the illicits. (The third group, the prescription psychoactives used on a nonprescription basis, is ignored entirely.)

In fact, the sciences of pharmacology, psychology, pathology, and epidemiology tell us that the drug problem is a unity, not a duality (Lowinson, Ruiz, Millman, & Langrod, 1997; Winick, 1997). The natural history of drug use in individuals, highlighting a phenomenon called the "gateway effect" (Chen & Kandel, 1995; Focus, 1991; Henningfield, 1990; Jonas, 1997, p. 779; Keegan, 1991; National Institute of Drug Abuse [NIDA], 1993; New York State Division of Alcoholism and Alcohol Abuse [NYSDAAA], 1989) illustrates this reality as well.

The existence of the gateway effect shows clearly that, almost invariably starting in childhood (Centers for Disease Control and Prevention [CDCP], 1990), tobacco and alcohol are the drugs of first use for almost *all* eventual long-term users of any mood-altering psychoactive drug, regardless of whether it is an illicit drug or not. Thus, tobacco-alcohol-marijuana-heroin-cocaine-etc. form a continuum, not a duality. But the cognitive dissonance of most drug policy analysts prevents them from seeing it. The drug warriors among them continue to believe that if the drug war can somehow just be prosecuted more vigorously *victory* can surely be achieved someday (Califano, 1993; Cooper, 1997; Kleber et al., 1997; Nagourney, 1996; Rosenthal, 1990, 1993, 1996; Shea, 1997).

The third factor accounting for the never-ending nature of the drug war can be described as a state of mind occurring frequently among the drug warriors called variously "Don't confuse us with facts," or "data-free policy making." (This state of mind can be seen as a variant of drug-war-related cognitive dissonance.) The evidence on this point is presented below, as is that on the fourth factor, that it is in the interest of both of the megadrug merchants, the tobacco and alcohol industries, to maintain the drug war just as it is.

TABLE 7.1 Percentage of Whites, Blacks, and Hispanics Over the Age of 12 Reporting Use of Selected Drugs in the Past Month, 1996

Drug	White	Black	Hispanic
Marijuana	4.6	6.6	3.7
Cocaine (incl. crack)	0.8	1.0	1.1
Any illicit drug	6.1	7.5	5.2
Alcohol	54.2	41.9	43.1
Alcohol "binge" use	16.1	13.1	16.7
Cigarettes	29.8	30.4	24.7

SOURCE: Substance Abuse and Mental Health Services Administration (1997, Tables 13-18).

Fifth on the list of major reasons why the drug war will never end is the utter weakness of the so-called drug-policy reform movement. Like the drug warrior group, it is often afflicted with cognitive dissonance, data-free policy making, and, on occasion, racism, as well as an inability to appreciate the true nature of the drug problem (or, in many cases, that there even is a drug problem). Given this state of affairs, it can be safely said that "in the foreseeable future, the 'drug war' will never end." Let us consider these factors ad seriatim.

■ Racism and the Drug War

The drug war, whether consciously or unconsciously, is a politico-racist enterprise (Sklar, 1995). As noted above, the percentage use in each major ethnic group of the primary RMADs, illicit and otherwise, are similar among the several major ethnic groups in the United States (see Table 7.1). Thus the majority of illicit drug use in the United States is among Whites (see Table 7.2). Nevertheless, the drug

TABLE 7.2 Number[a] and Percentage[b], by Race of Respondents Over the Age of 12 Reporting Use of Selected Drugs in Past Month, 1994, 1995

	White		Black		Hispanic	
Drug	No.	%	No.	%	No.	%
Marijuana (1995)	7,507	78	1,398	14	770	8
Cocaine (incl. crack, 1995)	958	71	305	22	217	16
Any illicit drug (1995)	9,583	77	1,871	15	1,007	8
Heroin (use in past year, 1994)	113	41	116	41	51	18
Psychotherapeutics (1994)	2,167	85	201	8	184	7

SOURCES: *For marijuana, cocaine, and "any illicit drug":* Substance Abuse and Mental Health Services Administration (1996, Tables 1a, 6-8). *For heroin and psychotherapeutics used on a nonprescription basis:* Substance Abuse and Mental Health Services Administration (1995, Tables 2-4, 8, 17).
a. Number of users over the age of 12 in thousands.
b. Percentage by race of the total number of users of each drug.

war is waged almost entirely in Black and to a lesser extent Hispanic communities. Consequently, the majority of persons in prison and jail for drug-related offenses (a primary outcome of the drug war being imprisonment of certain illicit drug users and dealers) are non-White (see Tables 7.3 through 7.5).

Turning to a consideration of law enforcement procedures by drug rather than by person as noted above, in the United States most anti-drug-use statutes as they are applied to most people are decriminalized. For the most part, only those laws dealing with the sale and use of certain illicit drugs to and by a limited segment of the population *defined by skin color and ethnicity* are enforced.

It is ironic that because of its highly limited and selective targeting, even if drug war violence were useful in permanently changing human drug-use behavior, since it directly affects White users to a

TABLE 7.3 Percentages by Race of Federal Prisoners Serving Time for Drug Offenses[a] and of Respondents Over the Age of 12 Reporting Any Illicit Drug Use in Past Month

Race	Percentage of Total Federal Prisoners	Percentage of Total Age 12 and Over Reporting Any Illicit Drug Use, 1995
White and Hispanic	26	85
Black	74	15

SOURCES: Mauer and Huling (1995, Figure 1), Perkins (1994, Table 5.5, p. 58) and Substance Abuse and Mental Health Services Administration (1997, Tables 1a, 6).
a. Percentages by race are projected for 1992 and are the most recent figures available.

TABLE 7.4 Percentages by Race of State Prisoners Serving Time for Drug Offenses[a] and of Respondents Over the Age of 12 Reporting Any Illicit Drug Use in Past Month

Race	Percentage of Total Federal Prisoners	Percentage of Total Age 12 and Over Reporting Any Illicit Drug Use, 1995
White	10	77
Black	74	15
Hispanic	16	8

SOURCES: Mauer and Huling (1995, Table 6) and Substance Abuse and Mental Health Services Administration (1996, Tables 1a, 6).
a. Percentages by race are projected for 1992 and are the most recent figures available.

TABLE 7.5 Number and Percentage, by Race of Local Jail Prisoners Serving Time for Drug Offenses[a] and of Respondents Over the Age of 12 Reporting Any Illicit Drug in Past Month

Race	Total No.	Percentage of Local Jail Prisoners	Percentage of Age 12 and Over Reporting Any Illicit Drug Use, 1995
White	24,500	25	77
Black	47,040	48	15
Hispanic	24,500	25	8
Other	1,960	2	—

SOURCES: Mauer (1989) and Substance Abuse and Mental Health Services Administration (1996, Tables 1a, 6).
a. Figures are for 1989 and are the most recent figures available.

much lesser extent than it affects non-White users, the drug war could not possibly have much impact on illicit drug use in the U.S. population as a whole. That is, unless it were thought that by locking up non-Whites use among Whites could be controlled and reduced.

The drug war does serve to create a set of self-fulfilling prophecies that are central to the racism that is central to U.S. politics. For example, in a vicious downward spiral of thought, policy, and action, law enforcement efforts contain the outdoor, street illicit drug trade to non-White neighborhoods, even though the majority of use is among Whites. Thus politicians, when assailing the illegal drug trade are easily able to paint it "black" in the public mind, *without ever having to say so* in so many words, even though it must be primarily a White phenomenon.

The drug war as it is waged (along with education, employment, housing, health, and family policies) is central to maintaining the whole U.S. politico-racist mythology: Blacks, especially the men, are inferior, lazy, dumb, handout hooked, good-for-nothing criminals who deny "family values" and will do just about anything to avoid working.

The political forces that promote this view of Black society *will not* give up the drug war. Unfortunately, most of those political forces that do not promote this view of Black society *cannot* give up the drug war, because they cannot or do not want to comprehend its true nature (see the section in this chapter on the drug policy reform movement). The latter forces are thus trapped politically by its rhetoric. And no reform can be achieved.

◼ The Drug War and Cognitive Dissonance

Cognitive dissonance can be defined as follows:

> A state of mind in which two positions that would appear to most objective observers to be in conflict with each other are strongly held, the conflict is neither recognized nor resolved by the holder, and causes no mental discomfort to the holder.

Let us consider a set of examples serially and not necessarily in order of importance.

Suicide and Related Factors

Depending on how the counts are made, suicide is currently about the 10th leading cause of death in the United States. The most common method of committing suicide is with a firearm, used in about 60% of cases (Santangelo, 1997). Drug overdoses, including alcohol, are linked to slightly more than 10% of cases. Many, although not all, of the strongest drug warriors are also among the strongest opponents of any kind of effective gun control measures.

The Glamorization of Drugs

In a weekly radio address in October 1997, President Clinton "blamed pop culture for glamorizing illegal drug use" (*Nation Briefs*, 1997). What he did not mention is the *national* drug culture that does the following (Gitlin, 1990; Johnson, 1988; Jonas, 1997, p. 779):

- Promotes the use of tobacco and alcohol through a multi-billion-dollar advertising and promotion program.

- By the way over-the-counter drugs are sold, characterizes drugs of all types as instant problem solvers.

- Markets vitamin use (and they do come in pill form) as a painless way to a better you.

- Is supported by the heavy emphasis American medicine places on the use of drugs for dealing with health and disease problems of all kinds.

Drug Smuggling

When the smuggled drug is one of the illicits, even though interdiction has been shown not to work (Committee on Government Operations, 1990), the never-ending calls are for redoubling our efforts to end it (Rosenthal, 1990, 1996). But suppose the smuggled drug is tobacco, and the smuggling network *begins* rather than ends in this country. For example,

> the largest tobacco companies are selling billions of dollars [worth] of cigarettes each year to traders and dealers who funnel them into black markets in many countries, say law enforcement officials and participants in the trade. (Bonner & Drew, 1997, p. A1)

In that case, the story is on page 1 for one day, the drug warriors all happen to be on vacation at the same time, and its absence as a topic either for the op-ed pages or roaring addresses by politicians of all stripes is notable.

The Death of Princess Diana

It is commonly held that alcohol played a significant role, perhaps the determining role, in the death of Diana, Princess of Wales (Sancton & Edwards, 1997). And *Time* was certainly lit up about it. Yet on the back cover of the issue in which the story appeared was an advertisement for Dewar's scotch and the very next page after the biography of the lead author on the alcohol-and-Di's-death story was a full-page advertisement for Cockborn's port. (Interestingly enough, on the page opposite the biography of the lead author on the alcohol-killed-Di story was a full-page advertisement for Benson & Hedges cigarettes, with the heading "Moonlight and Romance.") The story about the tragedy was not accompanied by calls for immediate reimposition of alcohol prohibition worldwide. But one wonders what the take would have been had the driver for the fatal journey been snorting cocaine instead of snifting *pastis*.

The Drug War Has Never Been Done Right

Many a drug warrior holds that the problem with the drug war and the reason why there is still a significant national drug problem after all these "war" years is that it simply has never been done the right way. For example,

> In a speech to a standing-room audience of students at the John F. Kennedy School of Government at Harvard University, [New York City Mayor Rudolph Giuliani] said that the problem of drug abuse has never been addressed in a comprehensive way. . . . [H]e said the [New York City] Police Department would step up its enforcement effort against drug dealers in an expansion of existing programs in northern Manhattan, the Bushwick section of Brooklyn, and the South Bronx . . . the city would increase drug treatment programs, and the school system would begin a comprehensive education program against drugs. (Firestone, 1997, p. B4)

What Mayor Giuliani detailed is in fact the national drug war program that has been under way since the Bush administration began it in 1989. With no indication that his program would or could possibly differ from the national program in its major emphasis on law enforcement, the mayor specified minority neighborhoods for increased police activity, did not indicate how treatment programs would deal with the drug problem at the population level, and failed to tell his listeners how his comprehensive anti-drug school education program would differ from the one already in place. And, as previously noted, the drug war's own documents tell us that it has not in any case achieved the goal it set for itself of controlling street drug availability. But this mayor is somehow going to "get it right" this time.

Demonization and Nondemonization

For the drug warrior, the drug dealer is the lowest of the low, luring his unsuspecting victim into a sure lifetime of sin and degradation. (The fact is that most persons who try an illicit drug other than marijuana do not go on to become regular users [SAMHSA, 1997], ~~but why confuse ourselves with facts?~~) "Snakes," "devils," and "criminals of the worst kind" are terms of approbation commonly applied to dealers in illicit drugs.

But tobacco merchants? Hardly demons, even though nicotine is a drug, unlike cocaine for example, that hooks most of those who try it (SAMHSA, 1997). Put aside the fact that nowhere are the tobacco merchants characterized as the prime accessories to 430,000 deaths per year that they are, simply for doing what they do. But even subterfuge by these people on a grand scale brings forth no cries of "snake" and "devil." Consider the following:

> A state judge here today released decades of secret tobacco industry documents that reflect discussions among cigarette company lawyers to suppress scientific research, potentially destroy documents and mislead the public about the health effects of smoking. (Meier, 1997)

Screams of anguish and condemnation of the individuals and corporations who perpetrated this highly lethal and expensive fraud upon the American public? Not commonly heard.

Heroin Use Is a Major Problem

"Heroin use is a major problem," compared with what? In September 1997, Alan I. Leshner, Director of the National Institute of Drug Abuse, convened a national meeting to "confront heroin use before it poses a genuine crisis" (Wren, 1997b). Leshner pointed out that in 1996 there were 141,000 new heroin users, whereas drug czar General Barry McCaffrey estimated that all told there were 600,000 heroin users in the United States, and called heroin "clearly one of the most intractable of all drugs to deal with."

Fascinating—in the same year there were over 70% as many deaths from tobacco use as there were total users of heroin. Yet, for heroin use, the prescription is the drug war, whereas under the proposed national settlement with the killer tobacco industry, the prescription is to let it off the liability hook really cheap and provide more education (Kessler, 1997).

What Works and What Does Not

Any truly effective national policy for dealing with all the RMADs must begin with the drugs that the users start with (almost invariably before the age of 21): tobacco and alcohol. It must recognize the whole gateway effect, the one that starts with tobacco and alcohol, not just the intermediate stage from marijuana onward. But the data on the health and social harms of illicit drug use are never placed in the context of the much greater health and social harms caused by tobacco and alcohol. And the drug warriors never recognize the success that has been achieved in reducing heavily promoted tobacco use without invoking anything like the drug war.

Finally, if prohibition is right for the illicits, why is it not right for tobacco and alcohol? The drug warriors' answer to this question comes down to the fact that both tobacco and alcohol are widely used and that, when tried, alcohol prohibition did not work anyway (Kleber et al., 1997, p. 859). (Neither for that matter did cigarette smoking prohibition, in effect in 15 states between 1895 and 1921 [National Commission on Marihuana and Drug Abuse, 1972].) These intellectual and policy contradictions and discordances are all a result of the widespread cognitive dissonance that afflicts drug policy analysts and makers of all stripes. It shows no signs of disappearing any time soon.

■ "Don't Confuse Me With Facts" or "Data-Free Policy Making"

Marijuana Does Not Have Any Medically Indicated Uses

In an October 13, 1997 *New York Times* article, it was noted that,

President Clinton's drug czar, retired Gen. Barry McCaffrey, has scoffed at the idea that marijuana is medically indicated. It is unnecessary, he wrote last month, because its active ingredient, THC [tetrahydrocannabinol], is synthesized and available as a prescription drug, Marinol. 'The argument that this chemical needs to be smoked . . . doesn't make sense.'

But numerous patients who have tried Marinol and found it ineffective report having benefited from [smoked] marijuana. It may be that the vapor form of the THC is more readily absorbed by the body, or that the smoke contains other ingredients not yet known. (Lewis, 1997, p. A15)

But let us not be confused by the facts when condemning thousands of people to lives filled with severe pain when they could have significantly less of it because "we don't want to set a bad example for our children" (says a drug warrior as he settles down, with his boys, to a Sunday afternoon of pro football and beer ads on his television set).

Simple Availability and Drug Use

The drug warriors commonly tell us that the most important reason for continuing the drug war is that ending it will immediately send the use of the illicits skyrocketing (Kleber et al., 1997, p. 856; Rosenthal, 1993). So do certain self-styled "reformers." A group of drug policy analysts and former drug policymakers formed in summer 1997 to attempt to "stake out the middle ground in the drug debate" (Wren, 1997a) said, "We cannot escape our current predicament by ending prohibition or legalizing drugs."

Lifting controls, they contended, could increase drug use. Again, it simply would not do to let the facts get in the way of statements like this one. Rather, why not simply ignore the fact that there is no historical evidence that simple availability in the absence of promotion leads to drug use (Jonas, 1997, p. 780). In fact, the historical evidence leads one to conclude that simple availability does *not* lead to increased drug use, that some other factors are necessary if that is to occur.

For example, it took about 80 years from the time of the invention of the automatic cigarette-making machine in 1885 and 60 years from the time of the perfection of the safety match around 1905 for per capita cigarette consumption to peak in the United States. It took about 35 years from the end of Prohibition for beer consumption to reach its 1919 level. According to the simple availability argument, it should not have taken anywhere near those periods of time for those increases in use to have taken place. And according to the drug warriors' simple-availability-leads-to-use theory, the Andean countries should be awash in cocaine addiction and Afghanistan should be awash in heroin addiction. They aren't.

This evidence shows clearly that availability *alone* does not cause widespread use. In addition, there is the evidence cited earlier in this chapter that significant *declines* in the use of both tobacco and cocaine have taken place in the face of ample supply of each. But why should the supply/use shibboleth not continue to be shouted from the rooftops, if its users really believe it to be true? No one ever said that addictions are both difficult to overcome and powerful stimuli to action.

Interdiction Is the Answer

According to an October 25, 1997 article in the *New York Times*,

> Deepening its involvement in a country that it has held at arm's length for years, the United States has approved sending more than $50 million in equipment to help Colombia's government fight guerillas involved in drug trafficking in the south. (Schemo, 1997, p. A1)

Back in 1990, after an extensive study of interdiction, the House of Representatives Government Operations Committee Report had this to say about that effort:

> The Andean Initiative reflects a largely military and law enforcement response to deep-rooted and diverse economic problems. . . . Source-country supply reduction programs for eradication, interdiction and enforcement have been ineffective in reducing the cultivation of coca or the available supply of coca products for processing or export in the Andean region. . . .
>
> Source-country interdiction and enforcement efforts have also been largely unsuccessful in curbing the amount of coca or coca products available for processing and export. Interdiction strategies in 1989 resulted in the seizure of less than one percent of all coca

paste and base produced in Peru, and only one half of one percent of Bolivian coca products.

There is no evidence to indicate that the situation has changed as of the mid-1990s (Fratello, 1994). But once again, let us not impose facts upon policy making when it comes to prosecuting the drug war.

The Swiss Experience Shows the Dangers of Legalization

In the early 1990s, the Swiss government commenced a program of legal distribution of heroin to people who could demonstrate that they were already addicted to the drug.

> A three-year study released in July [1997] showed a big drop in crime among addicts on the program, a huge improvement in their health, an increase in the number of those with steady housing and jobs and promising signs that some would try to kick the habit. With 30,000 addicts, Switzerland has one of the highest rates in Europe. But unlike [in] many countries, the death toll is falling. (Combined News Services, 1997)

On September 28, 1997, by a margin of almost 3 to 1, Swiss voters rejected an attempt by a group called Youth Without Drugs (YWD) to end the program. A YWD spokesman said, "To distribute heroin is the equivalent of a legal death." Apparently, Swiss drug warriors are no less engaged in data-free policy making than are their U.S. counterparts.

Needle Exchange, HIV Incidence, and Illicit Drug Use

A common and very dangerous complication of intravenous drug use (IDU) is the spread of Human Immunodeficiency Virus (HIV) infection through the use of contaminated injection syringes and needles by more than one person (DesJarlais, 1997). Programs promoting the use of clean needles and syringes either through "needle exchange" of injection equipment used once or making clean injection equipment readily available have shown that "both background [HIV] seroprevalence and the new infection rates are generally much lower in areas that permit over-the-counter sales of sterile injection equipment [one form of 'needle exchange']" (DesJarlais, 1997, p. 593).

Opponents of needle exchange programs often claim that among other things they will lead to an increase in intravenous drug use (General Accounting Office [GAO], 1993, p. 3). However, a review of studies of needle exchange programs by the GAO (1993) stated that "all five [studies meeting the GAO criteria for validity] found that drug use did not increase among users" (p. 3).

At the same time, while there was some evidence, not conclusive however, that needle exchange did not lead to an increase in the number of drug users, there was no evidence of any kind that it did lead to such an increase. Also there is evidence that needle exchange programs "have become important sources of referral to drug-misuse treatment programs" (DesJarlais, 1997, p. 594).

The response of a dedicated drug warrior like Gary Bauer, former Domestic Policy Advisor to President Ronald Reagan and currently president of the Family Research Council in Washington, to even the vaguest prospect that needle exchange programs might be expanded as part of the nationwide campaign against the spread of HIV infection and AIDS is instructive (Family Research Council News [FRC], August 20, 1997): "FRC President Gary L. Bauer said Wednesday that NEPs [needle exchange programs] 'are nothing but a Band-Aid on a bullet wound. The only way to stop the spread of HIV/AIDS among intravenous drug users is to step up the war on drugs.'" Once again, so much for data.

As long as the drug warriors stick to data-free policy making, and there is no indication that they will abandon it any time soon, there is no indication that the drug war will be abandoned any time soon either.

■ The Interests of the Megadrug Merchants

Next, the major RMAD industries in the United States, tobacco and alcohol, have a major interest in maintaining the drug war. As noted above, the sales of their products to underage people are illegal. It happens that underage people constitute almost all of those industries' potential new users. The drug war serves to divert attention from the illegal activities of the tobacco and alcohol industries, activities which happen, as noted, to be largely decriminalized. If there were no drug war as it is now conducted there might be much more focus on the illegal activities of the two major drug industries and possibly widespread public demands to take action against them. (The pharmaceutical industry too benefits from a drug war that diverts attention from the other decriminalized illegal drug market— that of prescription psychoactive drugs used on a nonprescription basis.)

The reason why the tobacco industry is so deathly afraid of FDA regulation of its product is not the programmatic content of the proposed regulations dealing with teenage smoking. That content is very similar to what the industry has already proposed. Rather, it is the proposed labeling of nicotine as an addictive drug and categorization of the cigarette as a "drug delivery device." Given the anti-drug climate in this country created by the drug war, if nicotine in tobacco comes to somehow be lumped with the illicits in the public consciousness, its days of acceptance would be numbered indeed.

■ The Ineffective Drug Policy Reform Movement

Finally, among the reasons accounting for the fact that the drug war will never end, it should be noted that the "drug policy reform movement" is completely ineffective. Primarily that is because it is married to (and presumably primarily funded by) right-wing libertarianism (Cato Policy Forum, 1994; Trebach & Zeese, 1992). The reformers therefore do not deal with the very real U.S. drug problem, the one that is responsible for over one fourth of all deaths (primarily from tobacco use) and (along with unregulated guns, also protected by right-wing libertarianism) a great deal of the violence, lethal and otherwise (significantly related to alcohol use) found in U.S. society. That is because libertarianism regards tobacco and alcohol use as matters of "free choice" (Goodman, 1991) beyond the purview of any national program to deal with it (an approach that would certainly require strong government intervention, anathema to the libertarians).

Furthermore, the reformers do not deal with the major causative factors for drug use in the United States, such as the drug culture and the gateway drug effect. That is because any effective program to deal with either one would also require major government intervention. Like the drug warriors, the reform movement ignores the integral tobacco-alcohol-illicit drug linkage, robbing itself of a powerful weapon in any public health-based campaign to reduce the use of all drugs in our society.

But most important, like the drug warriors, the reform movement treats the drug war as if it were *aracial*. Because it is anything but aracial, the reformers' nonracial approach cannot be useful. In fact, the reformers' approach does nothing but reinforce the drug warriors' artificially created twin fictions that drug use is primarily a Black problem but the drug war itself is aracial. Because illicit drug use is primarily a White problem and the drug war is in fact a racist enterprise to its core, a reform policy that does not recognize those facts cannot develop the highly sophisticated programmatic and political strategy that would be necessary to bring it to an end (as well as seriously deal with the real U.S. drug problem at the same time).

Finally, however correctly it is applied, the primary analytical and rhetorical tool of certain intellectual drug war opponents, simple logic (Nadelmann, 1989), simply cannot work in this total socio-political environment. Nor are either the reformers or the drug warriors interested in even discussing a comprehensive approach to dealing with the drug problem as a unity based in tried-and-true public health measures (Jonas, 1997).

In contrast with the drug war, effectiveness of the public health approach to the drug problem has already been demonstrated in the decline in cigarette smoking resulting from a modest anti-smoking campaign in the context of a highly addictive drug the dosage of which has been consistently manipulated by the sellers, the maintenance of infinite availability in relation to demand, and heavy promotion of use of the drug.

Implementation on a national scale of such a public health program aimed at the use of *all* RMADs could achieve the vital public health goal of significantly reducing the use of all drugs by all drug users. But there are too many powerful political and economic interests dead set against that approach and that outcome. Thus the public health approach to the drug problem does not stand a chance of being implemented.

In the end, for all these reasons, there is no end in sight for the drug war.

◼ Note

1. History has repeatedly demonstrated the failure of supply-side approaches to controlling recreational mood-altering drug availability, unless the drug in question can physically be completely eliminated from the marketplace.

This happened to be the case for beer during U.S. Prohibition (Lender & Martin, 1982; Rorabaugh, 1979). It was not the case for spirits, the supply and consumption of which were affected hardly at all by Prohibition (Lender & Martin, 1982; Rorabaugh, 1979). It takes a lot of space to make any significant quantities of beer. As well, most people need to drink a significant amount of the stuff in order to feel its effects. Therefore, beer can be termed a "large volume" drug carrier. Its use shrank to next to nothing during Prohibition. But the illicits produce their effects with the use of quite small volumes. Thus, like spirits were during Prohibition even to the likes of Elliott Ness, they are physically beyond the reach of the drug war.

◼ References

Bloom, F. E. (1997). The science of substance abuse. *Science, 278,* 15.

Bonner, R., & Drew, C. (1997, August 25). Cigarette makers are seen as aiding rise in smuggling: Tobacco giants deny role in illegal trade: Inquiries show there may be one. *New York Times,* p. A1.

Califano, J. (1993, December 15). No, fight harder. *New York Times.*

Cato Policy Forum. (1994, May/June). *Criminogenics: How the drug war causes crime* (Vol. 16, No. 3). Cato Policy Forum (CPF): Author.

Centers for Disease Control and Prevention. (1990). Survey of state and local laws on tobacco sales. *Morbidity and Mortality Weekly Reports, 39,* 349-352.

Chen, K., & Kandel, D. B. (1995). The natural history of drug use. *American Journal of Public Health, 85,* 41.

Combined News Services. (1997, September 29). Swiss back drugs for addicts policy. *Newsday.*

Committee on Government Operations, House of Representatives. (1990). *United States antinarcotics activities in the Andean region* (Union Calendar No. 584). Washington, DC: Government Printing Office.

Cooper, M. (1997, October 2). Giuliani announces a program to reduce illegal drug use. *New York Times*, p. B1.

DesJarlais, D. C. (1997). Epidemiology and emerging public health perspectives. In J. H. Lowinson, P. Ruiz, R. B. Millman, & J. G. Langrod (Eds.), *Substance abuse: A comprehensive textbook* (chap. 58). Baltimore, MD: Williams & Wilkins.

Duke. S. (1995, Winter). Drug prohibition: An unnatural disaster. *Connecticut Law Review, 27*(2).

Family Research Council News. (1997, August 20). *Americans overwhelmingly oppose needle exchange programs, say government should promote drug abstinence and rehab programs.* Washington, DC: Author.

Firestone, D. (1997, September 30). Offering a glimpse of a 2nd term, Giuliani vows a war on drugs. *New York Times*, p. B4.

Focus. (1991, January/February). *Alcohol: The gateway drug* (Vol. 6, No. 1). New York: New York Division of Alcoholism and Alcohol Abuse.

Fratello, D. (1994, Fall). Listening to cocaine. *Drug Policy Letter*, p. 11.

General Accounting Office. (1993, March). *Needle exchange programs* (GAO/HRD9360). Washington, DC: Author.

Gitlin, T. (1990). On drugs and mass media in America's consumer society. In H. Resnik (Ed.), *Youth and drugs: Society's mixed messages*. Rockville, MD: Office of Substance Abuse Prevention.

Goldstein, P. J., Brownstein, H. H., Ryan, P. J., & Bellucci, P. A. (1990, March/April). Most drug-related murders result from crack sales, not use. *Drug Policy Letter, 2*(2), 6.

Goodman, R. (1991). Public health proposals are a bad way to try ending prohibition. *Drug Policy Letter, 3*(4), 14-15.

Greenberg, J. (1990, September 3). All about crime. *New York Times*, p. 20.

Henningfield, J. (1990, Autumn). Smokeless tobacco: Addictive and a gateway drug. *Tobacco and Youth Reporter*, p. 11.

Institute for Health Policy, Brandeis University. (1993). *Substance abuse: The nation's number one health problem. Key indicators for policy*. Princeton, NJ: Robert Wood Johnson Foundation.

Johnson, W. O. (1988, August 8). Sports and suds. *Sports Illustrated*, p. 68.

Jonas, S. (1997). Public health approaches. In J. H. Lowinson, P. Ruiz, R. B. Millman, & J. G. Langrod (Eds.), *Substance abuse: A comprehensive textbook* (chap. 77). Baltimore, MD: Williams & Wilkins.

Keegan, A. (1991, Summer/Fall). Tobacco may provide gateway to drug, alcohol abuse. *NIDA Notes*, p. 23.

Kessler, D. (1997). The tobacco settlement. *New England Journal of Medicine, 337*, 1082.

Kleber, H. D., Califano, J. A., & Demers, J. C. (1997). Clinical and societal implications of drug legalization. In M. E. Lender & J. K. Martin (Eds.), *Drinking in America: A history* (pp. 196-197). New York: Free Press.

Lender, M. E., & Martin, J. K. (1982). *Drinking in America: A history.* New York: The Free Press.

Lewis, A. (1997, October 13). Medicine and politics. *New York Times,* p. A15.

Lowinson, J. H., Ruiz, P., Millman, R. B., & Langrod, J. G. (Eds.). (1997). *Substance abuse: A comprehensive textbook.* Baltimore: Williams & Wilkins.

MacCoun, R., & Reuter, P. (1997). Interpreting Dutch cannabis policy, reasoning by analogy in the legalization debate. *Science, 278,* p. 47.

Mauer, M. (1989). *Drugs and jail inmates.* Washington, DC: Bureau of Justice Statistics.

Mauer, M., & Huling, T. (1995, October). *Young Black Americans and the criminal justice system.* Washington, DC: Sentencing Project.

McGinniss, J. M., & Foege, W. H. (1993). Actual causes of death in the United States. *Journal of the American Medical Association, 270,* 2207.

Meier, B. (1997, August 7). Tobacco lawyers' papers are made public. *New York Times.*

Nadelmann, E. (1989). Drug prohibition in the United States: Costs, consequences, and alternatives. *Science, 245,* 939-947.

Nagourney, A. (1996, September 19). Attacking drugs, Dole takes on the entertainment industry. *New York Times,* p. B10.

Nation Briefs. (1997, October 12). Clinton: Drugs glamorized. *Newsday.*

National Commission on Marihuana and Drug Abuse. (1972). *Marihuana: A signal of misunderstanding.* Washington, DC: Government Printing Office.

National Drug Control Strategy. (1997, February). *The national drug control strategy, 1997.* Washington, DC: Author.

National Institute of Drug Abuse. (1993). *Tobacco as a gateway drug* (chart). New York: Smoke-Free Educational Services.

New York State Division of Alcoholism and Alcohol Abuse. (1989). *Alcohol: The gateway to other drug use.* Buffalo, NY: Research Institute on Alcoholism. (See this publication for a comprehensive bibliography on the gateway drug effect.)

Perkins, C. (1994). *National corrections report program, 1991.* Washington, DC: Bureau of Justice Statistics.

Rorabaugh, W. J. (1979). *The alcoholic republic: An American tradition* (pp. 233, 290-293). New York: Oxford University Press.

Rosenthal, A. M. (1990, December 10). Surrender on drugs? *New York Times.*

Rosenthal, A. M. (1993, May 18). Dismantling the war. *New York Times,* p. A2.

Rosenthal, A. M. (1996, October 22). Job for a president. *New York Times.*

Substance Abuse and Mental Health Services Administration. (1995). *National Household Survey on Drug Abuse: Population estimates 1994.* (DHHS Pub. No. SMA 953063). Rockville, MD: U.S. Department of Health and Human Services.

Substance Abuse and Mental Health Services Administration. (1996). *Preliminary estimates from the 1995 National Survey on Drug Abuse.* Rockville, MD: U.S. Department of Health and Human Services.

Substance Abuse and Mental Health Services Administration. (1997). *Preliminary results from the 1996 Household Survey on Drug Abuse* (DHHS Pub. No. SMA 973149). Rockville, MD: U.S. Department of Health and Human Services, SAMHSA Office of Applied Statistics.

Sancton, T., & Edwards, T. M. (1997, September 22). Drunk and drugged: The shocking tale of how Diana's driver spent the hours before her death. *Time*, p. 27.

Santangelo, M. (1997, August 29). Suicide: West is worst. *Newsday*, p. A23.

Schemo, D. J. (1997, October 25). U.S. is to help army in Colombia fight drugs but skeptics abound. *New York Times*, p. A1.

Shannon, E. (1990, December 3). A losing battle. *Time*, p. 44.

Shea, C. (1997, October 3). In drug-policy debates, a center at Columbia U. takes a hard line. *Chronicle of Higher Education*, p. A15.

Sklar, H. (1995, December). Reinforcing racism with the war on drugs. *Z Magazine*, p. 19.

Trebach, A. S., & Zeese, K. B. (1992). *Milton Friedman and Thomas Szasz: On liberty and drugs*. Washington, DC: Drug Policy Foundation Press.

Winick, C. (1997). Epidemiology. In J. H. Lowinson, P. Ruiz, R. B. Millman, & J. G. Langrod (Eds.), *Substance abuse: A comprehensive textbook*. Baltimore, MD: Williams & Wilkins.

Wren, C. S. (1997a, September 1). New voice in drug debate seeks to lower the volume. *New York Times*.

Wren, C. S. (1997b, September 30). U.S. convenes experts on drugs to grapple with heroin use. *New York Times*.

War Is Still
Not the Answer

KARST J. BESTEMAN

resident Nixon was the first elected leader of the country to declare war on drugs. He did this in 1971 with a strong law enforcement initiative against drug traffickers and major dealers and with a rapid expansion of drug treatment programs focused on heroin addiction. Presidents Ford, Carter, Reagan, Bush, and Clinton continued the effort, with each promising to increase the war effort against drugs but with different priorities.

The nature of the federal role in international interdiction activities has led to the promise of more potent weapons, faster pursuit crafts, and greater bilateral cooperation. As an afterthought to these commitments each administration has mentioned the importance of reducing the demand for drugs. The specific actions that will result in a reduction of demand are not described with any detail.

151

In examining this emphasis and its 25-year history, it is my conclusion that the "War on Drugs" is not the answer to the many problems of drug abuse in this country. I reach this conclusion by observing that during the entire time the country has been at war against drugs there has been no attempt in any administration to place the federal agencies and the American people on a wartime status. There are several characteristics of a country at war that have not been met. These characteristics are as follows:

- Total mobilization
- Use of unlimited resources
- Use of expendable personnel and willingness to take casualties
- Strategic leadership by professionals
- A national commitment to victory at any cost

Drug abuse is not monolithic. It is not the problem or a problem to be solved. Drug abuse manifests itself in a multitude of problems. Some of these drug problems are the direct result of the physiological impact of the drug, and some are the result of psychological impairment and decrement of performance. Virtually none of the direct drug effects cause an urgent response from our society. Urgency is generated by the nature of problems associated with drug abuse.

There is an acute social concern about driving a vehicle while under the influence of a drug. Drugged drivers are subject to a number of punitive measures designed to assure the safety of the motoring public. People become upset with the seemingly random and unprovoked violence that is associated with the distribution of illicit drugs. Communities now keep score of homicides as "drug related." Drug abuse is viewed as the cause of family dysfunction and disruption. Drug abuse is condemned as a cause of damaged newborns.

An entire industry has developed to control and remove drug abuse from the workplace. Preemployment testing, laboratory standards, for-cause testing, and false positives have become an important part of discussions for employers. Congress has passed legislative proposals to test employees who are part of the nation's transportation system. Industry is concerned about potential losses in productivity due to reduced and impaired capacity of workers.

Local communities and courts are angered and overwhelmed at the realization that addicted criminals are likely to escalate the number of criminal acts fivefold over their criminal activity during periods when not addicted. Surveys by arresting authorities repeatedly report that over 60% of the suspects arrested and arraigned test positive for the presence of illicit drugs.

Periodically, reports make us aware that law enforcement officials, bankers, and other highly respected community leaders have been corrupted by the large amounts of money that fuel drug trafficking. Corruption in the United States remains largely underreported as blatant corruption in supplier and transshipment nations becomes a media focus.

As all these factors accumulate, public policy discussion seems frozen in a repetitive pattern. Legislators, expressing frustration, reflexively seek to pass more punitive and restrictive laws. Strident rhetoric is the norm. The ineffectiveness of previously enacted criminal sanctions to deter the use of and trafficking in illicit drugs is used as the reason to pass more stringent laws as a primary strategy to accomplish the policy goal of zero tolerance. This repetitious legislative and political ritual continues in the face of research that indicates that certain and swift punishment have a greater impact on changing behavior than the threat of severe punishment.

In my opinion, the United States has passed the point of benefit from increased criminal penalties. Continued reliance on increased criminal penalties will prove useless. It is time to consider that many of the problems of drug abuse do not respond to combat strategies but can be solved by engaging in a concerted public health approach. This is not a mystery. It requires patience. It requires much more precise information to craft an effective response.

If the country is to change its response to drug abuse and the associated problems it must improve the accuracy and appropriateness of its data. The federal government uses essentially three major indicators to monitor illicit drug consumption. They are the High School Senior Survey, the Household Survey, and the Drug Abuse Warning Network. Each of these data sets serves a limited purpose. None defines the extent or nature of the drug use and drug-related problems in our society. There is no comparably inadequate estimate of any other health issue in the U.S. Public Health Service. The excuse given by federal agencies for not mounting a more adequate effort to define the scope and nature of drug abuse is cost. Yet the federal government is spending billions of dollars each year without an adequate problem definition to plan effective interventions.

The technical skill exists to accomplish this task. Specific drug abuse patterns and the associated problems can be defined and quantified. Our national public policy leaders within the federal government prefer to approach these issues from a position of ignorant common sense. This leads to the charade by both the administration and Congress in generating solutions to unknown and undefined problems. Congress bears a major responsibility for this situation by not developing intensive oversight hearings with substantial effort to elicit testimony from the most expert witnesses to develop the background information for effective legislation. During nonelection years, congressional committees claim that drug abuse issues are not urgent enough or of a high enough priority for committees to use their valuable time to develop legislation. During election years, legislation is frequently rushed through the process with only minimal public testimony to assure a concerned electorate that something is being done about these serious problems.

Agencies within the executive branch of government acknowledge the deficiencies of their information. They are hesitant to propose adequate data collection, preferring instead to demonstrate their effectiveness and to justify next year's appropriation by activities that show that the agency is taking action toward solving the problems of drug abuse. There is little incentive to be self-critical. There is little incentive to evaluate existing programs. There is a strong reliance on the premise that the agency would not exist if it were not carrying out needed activities to suppress drug abuse.

How would changing our national approach to drug abuse and its associated problems bring about a more effective response from our federal government? Taking a public health approach would necessitate a complete reexamination of all our current activities and would force the country to broaden the scope of response.

First, a public health problem is the responsibility of the public. As defined today, drug abuse is essentially a criminal enterprise. Criminal activities are the responsibility of law enforcement agencies.

As a public, we report crime. We do not intervene. We do not enforce the law. We are instructed to stand aside and allow the police to perform their duty. With a public health approach each of us has a role. It may be only admonition or instruction, but we are responsible for ourselves and our families in a primary manner.

A public health approach encourages separating small segments of drug abuse and its associated problems to accomplish incremental change. Lethal overdose by contaminated illicit drugs can be reduced through targeted information and education efforts. To the extent that many drug overdose episodes are the result of drug combinations and interactions, information regarding the synergistic effect of alcohol with other drugs both licit and illicit can be widely disseminated. This is particularly useful when discussing the effect of alcohol combined with some frequently used prescription medications.

A public health approach would allow for a stronger scientific base for program response. Marijuana is again, as it was in the late 1960s, a contentious policy issue. By recognizing that marijuana is not a lethal drug and setting aside the legal arguments over classification, the discussion can focus on the benefits and risks of use, abuse, and addiction. This information will have implications for public policy. Today with the contention regarding the proper classification of marijuana, there is little opportunity to address activities that would reduce the rate of its use by young people.

The prohealth lifestyle movement is an outgrowth of the understanding that public health is the sum of a vast number of individual decisions and actions. The public has demonstrated its responsiveness to improving health practices. The public has not demonstrated its approval of the war against inanimate substances. The public needs to understand the connection between an action required and an outcome desired.

There are several other features of the public health approach that, if followed, would assist the nation's leaders and the public in selecting an agreed-upon goal with specific strategies for solution. The focus of public health is to understand with great precision how and why a disease spreads. There is great emphasis on how an individual can avoid illness. Failing to avoid the illness, intense study is given to raising resistance to the disease. In the event all else fails, there are major efforts to treat the illness.

None of these alternatives have been aggressively pursued during the past 25 years. Drug abuse has been defined as a character flaw, a moral failure, criminal, and a threat to the fabric of our society. War was declared. Drug abuse and its associated problems have not retreated. It is time for a fundamental reassessment of our national policies and approach. War against our own citizens is unthinkable. The war against drugs is unwon.

Until our elected leaders and their appointed officials who develop policy and execute programs abandon their reflexive reliance on hostile symbols, we will experience little progress in diminishing the problems of drug abuse. The individuals and groups who regularly abuse licit and illicit drugs have little motivation to engage the efforts to change and rejoin the greater community when every message from that community proclaims them as the enemy.

Commonsense
Drug Policy

ETHAN A. NADELMANN

■ First, Reduce Harm

In 1988 Congress passed a resolution proclaiming its goal of "a drug-free America by 1995." U.S. drug policy has failed persistently over the decades because it has preferred such rhetoric to reality, and moralism to pragmatism. Politicians confess their youthful indiscretions, then call for tougher drug laws. Drug control officials make assertions with no basis in fact or science. Police officers, generals, politicians, and guardians of public morals qualify as drug czars—but not, to date, a single doctor or public health figure. Independent commissions are appointed to evaluate drug policies, only to see their recommendations ignored as politically risky. And drug policies are

AUTHOR'S NOTE: Reprinted by permission of *Foreign Affairs*, Volume 77, No. 1, 1998. Copyright 1998 by the Council on Foreign Relations, Inc.

designed, implemented, and enforced with virtually no input from the millions of Americans they affect most—drug users. Drug abuse is a serious problem, both for individual citizens and society at large, but the "War on Drugs" has made matters worse, not better.

Drug warriors often point to the 1980s as a time in which the drug war really worked. Illicit drug use by teenagers peaked around 1980, then fell more than 50% over the next 12 years. During the 1996 presidential campaign, Republican challenger Bob Dole made much of the recent rise in teenagers' use of illicit drugs, contrasting it with the sharp drop during the Reagan and Bush administrations. President Clinton's response was tepid, in part because he accepted the notion that teen drug use is the principal measure of drug policy's success or failure; at best, he could point out that the level was still barely half what it had been in 1980.

In 1980, however, no one had ever heard of the cheap, smokable form of cocaine called crack, or drug-related HIV infection or AIDS. By the 1990s, both had reached epidemic proportions in American cities, largely driven by prohibitionist economics and morals indifferent to the human consequences of the drug war. In 1980, the federal budget for drug control was about $1 billion, and state and local budgets were perhaps two or three times that. By 1997, the federal drug control budget had ballooned to $16 billion, two thirds of it for law enforcement agencies, and state and local funding to at least that. On any day in 1980, approximately 50,000 people were behind bars for violating a drug law. By 1997, the number had increased eightfold, to about 400,000. These are the results of a drug policy overreliant on criminal justice "solutions," ideologically wedded to abstinence-only treatment, and insulated from cost-benefit analysis.

Imagine instead a policy that starts by acknowledging that drugs are here to stay, and that we have no choice but to learn how to live with them so that they cause the least possible harm. Imagine a policy that focuses on reducing not illicit drug use per se but the crime and misery caused by both drug abuse and prohibitionist policies. And imagine a drug policy based not on the fear, prejudice, and ignorance that drive America's current approach but rather on common sense, science, public health concerns, and human rights. Such a policy is possible in the United States, especially if Americans are willing to learn from the experiences of other countries where such policies are emerging.

■ Attitudes Abroad

Americans are not averse to looking abroad for solutions to the nation's drug problems. Unfortunately, they have been looking in the wrong places—Asia and Latin America, where much of the world's heroin and cocaine originates. Decades of U.S. efforts to keep drugs from being produced abroad and exported to American markets have failed. Illicit drug production is a bigger business than ever before. The opium poppy, source of morphine and heroin, and *cannabis saliva*, from which marijuana and hashish are prepared, grow readily around the world; the coca plant, from whose leaves cocaine is extracted, can be cultivated far from its native environment in the Andes. Crop substitution programs designed to persuade Third World peasants to grow legal crops cannot compete with the profits that drug prohibition makes inevitable. Crop eradication campaigns occasionally reduce production in one country, but new suppliers pop up elsewhere. International law enforcement efforts can disrupt drug trafficking organizations and routes, but they rarely have much impact on U.S. drug markets.

Even if foreign supplies could be cut off, the drug abuse problem in the United States would scarcely abate. Most of America's drug-related problems are associated with domestically produced alcohol and tobacco. Much if not most of the marijuana, amphetamine, hallucinogens, and illicitly diverted pharmaceutical drugs consumed in the country are made in the United States. The same is true of the glue, gasoline, and other solvents used by kids too young or too poor to obtain other psychoactive substances. No doubt such drugs, as well as new products, would quickly substitute for imported heroin and cocaine if the flow from abroad dried up.

While looking to Latin America and Asia for supply-reduction solutions to America's drug problems is futile, the harm-reduction approaches spreading throughout Europe and Australia and even into corners of North America show promise. These approaches start by acknowledging that supply-reduction initiatives are inherently limited, that criminal justice responses can be costly and counterproductive, and that single-minded pursuit of a "drug-free society" is dangerously quixotic. Demand-reduction efforts to prevent drug abuse among children and adults are important, but so are harm-reduction efforts to lessen the damage to those unable or unwilling to stop using drugs immediately, and to those around them.

Most proponents of harm reduction do not favor legalization. They recognize that prohibition has failed to curtail drug abuse, that it is responsible for much of the crime, corruption, disease, and death associated with drugs, and that its costs mount every year. But they also see legalization as politically unwise and as risking increased drug use. The challenge is thus making drug prohibition work better, but with a focus on reducing the negative consequences of both drug use and prohibitionist policies.

Countries that have turned to harm-reduction strategies for help in alleviating their drug woes are not so different from the United States. Drugs, crime, and race problems, and other socio-economic problems are inextricably linked. As in America, criminal justice authorities still prosecute and imprison major drug traffickers as well as petty dealers who create public nuisances. Parents worry that their children might get involved with drugs. Politicians remain fond of drug war rhetoric. But by contrast with U.S. drug policy, public health goals have priority, and public health authorities have substantial influence. Doctors have far more latitude in treating addiction and associated problems. Police view the sale and use of illicit drugs as similar to prostitution—vice activities that cannot be stamped out but can be effectively regulated. Moralists focus less on any inherent evils of drugs than on the need to deal with drug use and addiction pragmatically and humanely. And more politicians dare to speak out in favor of alternatives to punitive prohibitionist policies.

Harm-reduction innovations include efforts to stem the spread of HIV by making sterile syringes readily available and collecting used syringes; allowing doctors to prescribe oral methadone for heroin addiction treatment, as well as heroin and other drugs for addicts who would otherwise buy them on the black market; establishing "safe injection rooms" so addicts do not congregate in public places or dangerous "shooting galleries"; employing drug analysis units at the large dance parties called raves to test the quality and potency of MDMA, known as Ecstasy, and other drugs that patrons buy and consume there; decriminalizing (but not legalizing) possession and retail sale of cannabis and, in some cases, possession of small amounts of "hard" drugs; and integrating harm-reduction policies and principles into community policing strategies. Some of these measures are under way or under consideration in parts of the United States, but rarely to the extent found in growing numbers of foreign countries.

Stopping HIV With Sterile Syringes

The spread of HIV, the virus that causes AIDS, among people who inject drugs illegally was what prompted governments in Europe and Australia to experiment with harm-reduction policies. During the early 1980s public health officials realized that infected users were spreading HIV by sharing needles. Having already experienced a hepatitis epidemic attributed to the same mode of transmission, the Dutch were the first to tell drug users about the risks of needle sharing and to make sterile syringes available and collect dirty needles through pharmacies, needle exchange and methadone programs, and public health services. Governments elsewhere in Europe and in Australia soon followed suit. The few countries in which a prescription was necessary to obtain a syringe dropped the requirement. Local authorities in Germany, Switzerland, and other European countries authorized needle exchange machines to ensure 24-hour access. In some European cities, addicts can exchange used syringes for clean ones at local police stations without fear of prosecution or harassment. Prisons are instituting similar policies to help discourage the spread of HIV among inmates, recognizing that illegal drug injecting cannot be eliminated even behind bars.

These initiatives were not adopted without controversy. Conservative politicians argued that needle exchange programs condoned illicit and immoral behavior and that government policies should focus on punishing drug users or making them drug-free. But by the late 1980s, the consensus in most of Western Europe, Oceania, and Canada was that while drug abuse was a serious problem, AIDS was worse. Slowing the spread of a fatal disease for which no cure exists was the greater moral imperative. There was also a fiscal imperative. Needle exchange programs' costs are minuscule compared with those of treating people who would otherwise become infected with HIV.

Only in the United States has this logic not prevailed, even though AIDS was the leading killer of Americans ages 25 to 44 for most of the 1990s and is now number 2. The Centers for Disease

Control (CDC) estimates that half of new HIV infections in the country stem from injection drug use. Yet both the White House and Congress block allocation of AIDS or drug-abuse prevention funds for needle exchange, and virtually all state governments retain drug paraphernalia laws, pharmacy regulations, and other restrictions on access to sterile syringes. During the 1980s, AIDS activists engaging in civil disobedience set up more syringe exchange programs than state and local governments. There are now more than 100 such programs in 28 states, Washington, D.C., and Puerto Rico, but they reach only an estimated 10% of injection drug users.

Governments at all levels in the United States refuse to fund needle exchange for political reasons, even though dozens of scientific studies, domestic and foreign, have found that needle exchange and other distribution programs reduce needle sharing, bring hard-to-reach drug users into contact with health care systems, and inform addicts about treatment programs, yet do not increase illegal drug use. In 1991 the National AIDS Commission appointed by President Bush called the lack of federal support for such programs "bewildering and tragic." In 1993 a CDC-sponsored review of research on needle exchange recommended federal funding, but top officials in the Clinton administration suppressed a favorable evaluation of the report within the Department of Health and Human Services. In July 1996 President Clinton's Advisory Council on HIV/AIDS criticized the administration for its failure to heed the National Academy of Sciences' recommendation that it authorize the use of federal money to support needle exchange programs. An independent panel convened by the National Institute of Health reached the same conclusion in February 1997. In summer 1998, the American Medical Association, the American Bar Association, and even the politicized U.S. Conference of Mayors endorsed the concept of needle exchange. In fall 1998, an endorsement followed from the World Bank.

To date, America's failure in this regard is conservatively estimated to have resulted in the infection of up to 10,000 people with HIV. Mounting scientific evidence and the stark reality of the continuing AIDS crisis have convinced the public, if not politicians, that needle exchange saves lives; polls consistently find that a majority of Americans support needle exchange, with approval highest among those most familiar with the notion. Prejudice and political cowardice are poor excuses for allowing more citizens to suffer from and die of AIDS, especially when effective interventions are cheap, safe, and easy.

Methadone and Other Alternatives

The United States pioneered the use of the synthetic opiate methadone to treat heroin addiction in the 1960s and 1970s, but now lags behind much of Europe and Australia in making methadone accessible and effective. Methadone is the best available treatment in terms of reducing illicit heroin use and associated crime, disease, and death. In the early 1990s the National Academy of Sciences' Institute of Medicine stated that of all forms of drug treatment, "methadone maintenance has been the most rigorously studied modality and has yielded the most incontrovertibly positive results. . . . Consumption of all illicit drugs, especially heroin, declines. Crime is reduced, fewer individuals become HIV positive, and individual functioning is improved." However, the institute went on to declare, "Current policy . . . puts too much emphasis on protecting society from methadone, and not enough on protecting society from the epidemics of addiction, violence, and infectious diseases that methadone can help reduce."

Methadone is to street heroin what nicotine skin patches and chewing gum are to cigarettes—with the added benefit of legality. Taken orally, methadone has little of injected heroin's effect on mood or cognition. It can be consumed for decades with few if any negative health consequences, and its purity and concentration, unlike street heroin's, are assured. Like other opiates, it can create physical dependence if taken regularly, but the "addiction" is more like a diabetic's "addiction" to insulin than a heroin addict's to the product bought on the street. Methadone patients can and do drive safely, hold good jobs, and care for their children. When prescribed adequate doses, they can be indistinguishable from people who have never used heroin or methadone.

Popular misconceptions and prejudice, however, have all but prevented any expansion of methadone treatment in the United States. The 115,000 Americans receiving methadone today represent only a small increase over the number 20 years ago. For every 10 heroin addicts, there are only one or two methadone treatment slots.

Methadone is the most tightly controlled drug in the pharmacopoeia, subject to unique federal and state restrictions. Doctors cannot prescribe it for addiction treatment outside designated programs. Regulations dictate not only security, documentation, and staffing requirements but maximum doses, admission criteria, time spent in the program, and a host of other specifics, none of which has much to do with quality of treatment. Moreover, the regulations do not prevent poor treatment; many clinics provide insufficient doses, prematurely detoxify clients, expel clients for offensive behavior, and engage in other practices that would be regarded as unethical in any other field of medicine. Attempts to open new clinics tend to be blocked by residents who do not want addicts in their neighborhood.

In much of Europe and Australia, methadone treatment was at first even more controversial than in the United States; some countries, including Germany, France, and Greece, prohibited it well into the 1980s and 1990s. But where methadone has been accepted, doctors have substantial latitude in deciding how and when to prescribe it so as to maximize its efficacy. There are methadone treatment programs for addicts looking for rehabilitation and programs for those simply trying to reduce their heroin consumption. Doctors in regular medical practice can prescribe the drug, and patients fill their prescriptions at local pharmacies. Thousands of general practitioners throughout Europe, Australia, New Zealand, and Canada (notably in Ontario and British Columbia) are now involved in methadone maintenance. In Belgium, Germany, and Australia this is the principal means of distribution. Integrating methadone with mainstream medicine makes treatment more accessible, improves its quality, and allocates ancillary services more efficiently. It also helps reduce the stigma of methadone programs and community resistance to them.

Many factors prevent American doctors from experimenting with the more flexible treatment programs of their European counterparts. The Drug Enforcement Administration contends that looser regulations would fuel the illicit market in diverted methadone. But the black market, in which virtually all buyers are heroin addicts who cannot or will not enroll in methadone programs, is primarily a product of the inadequate legal availability of methadone. Some conventional providers do not want to cede their near-monopoly over methadone treatment and are reluctant to take on addicts who can't or won't commit to quitting heroin. And all efforts to make methadone more available in the United States run up against the many Americans who dismiss methadone treatment as substituting one addictive drug for another and are wary of any treatment that does not leave the patient "drug free."

Oral methadone works best for hundreds of thousands of heroin addicts, but some fare better with other opiate substitutes. In England, doctors prescribe injectable methadone for about 10% of recovering patients, who may like the modest "rush" upon injection or the ritual of injecting. Doctors in Austria, Switzerland, and Australia are experimenting with prescribing oral morphine to determine whether it works better than oral methadone for some users. Several treatment programs in the Netherlands have conducted trials with oral morphine and palfium. In Germany, where methadone treatment was initially shunned, thousands of addicts have been maintained on codeine, which many doctors and patients still prefer to methadone. The same is true of buprenorphine in France.

In England, doctors have broad discretion to prescribe whatever drugs help addicted patients manage their lives and stay away from illegal drugs and their dealers. Beginning in the 1920s, thousands of English addicts were maintained on legal prescriptions of heroin, morphine, amphetamine, cocaine, and other pharmaceutical drugs. This tradition flourished until the 1960s, and has reemerged in response to AIDS and to growing disappointment with the Americanization of British prescribing practices during the 1970s and 1980s, when illicit heroin use in Britain increased almost tenfold. Doctors in other European countries and Australia are also trying heroin prescription.

The Swiss government began a nationwide trial in 1994 to determine whether prescribing heroin, morphine, or injectable methadone could reduce crime, disease, and other drug-related ills. Some 1,000 volunteers took part in the experiment—only heroin addicts with at least two unsuccessful experiences in methadone or other conventional treatment programs were considered. The trial quickly determined that virtually all participants preferred heroin, and doctors subsequently prescribed it for them. In July 1997 the government reported the results so far: criminal offenses and the number of criminal offenders dropped 60%, the percentage of income from illegal and semilegal activities fell from 69% to 10%, illegal heroin *and* cocaine use declined dramatically (although use of alcohol, cannabis, and tranquilizers like Valium remained fairly constant), stable employment increased from 14% to 32%, physical health improved enormously, and most participants greatly reduced their contact with the drug scene. There were no deaths from overdoses, and no prescribed drugs were diverted to the black market. More than half of those who dropped out of the study switched to another form of drug treatment, including 83 who began abstinence therapy. A cost-benefit analysis of the program found a net economic benefit of $30 per patient per day, mostly because of reduced criminal justice and health care costs.

The Swiss study has undermined several myths about heroin and its habitual users. The results to date demonstrate that, given relatively unlimited availability, heroin users will voluntarily stabilize or reduce their dosage and some will even choose abstinence; that long-addicted users can lead relatively normal, stable lives if provided legal access to their drug of choice; and that ordinary citizens will support such initiatives. In recent referendums in Zurich, Basel, and Zug, substantial majorities voted to continue funding local arms of the experiment. In September of 1997, a nationwide referendum to end the government's heroin maintenance and other harm-reduction initiatives was rejected by 71% of Swiss voters, including majorities in all 26 cantons.

The Netherlands participated in its own heroin prescription study in 1998, and similar trials are under consideration elsewhere in Europe, including Luxembourg and Spain, as well as Canada. In Germany, the federal government has opposed heroin prescription trials and other harm-reduction innovations, but the League of Cities has petitioned it for permission to undertake them; a survey early last year found that police chiefs in 10 of the country's 12 largest cities favored letting states implement controlled heroin distribution programs. In Australia in 1997, a majority of state health ministers approved a heroin prescription trial, but Prime Minister John Howard blocked it. And in Denmark, a September 1996 poll found that 66% of voters supported an experiment that would provide registered addicts with free heroin to be consumed in centers set up for the purpose.

Switzerland, attempting to reduce overdoses, dangerous injecting practices, and shooting up in public places, has also taken the lead in establishing "safe-injection rooms" where users can inject their drugs under secure, sanitary conditions. There are now about a dozen such rooms in the country, and initial evaluations are positive. In Germany, Frankfurt has set up three, and there are also officially sanctioned facilities in Hamburg and Saarbrücken. Cities elsewhere in Europe and in Australia are expected to open safe injection rooms soon.

▄ Reefer Sanity

Cannabis, in the form of marijuana and hashish, is by far the most popular illicit drug in the United States. More than a quarter of Americans admit to having tried it. Marijuana's popularity peaked in 1980, dropped steadily until the early 1990s, and is now on the rise again. Although it is not entirely safe, especially when consumed by children, smoked heavily, or used when driving, it is clearly among the least dangerous psychoactive drugs in common use. In 1988 the administrative law judge for the Drug Enforcement Administration, Francis Young, reviewed the evidence and concluded that "marihuana, in its natural form, is one of the safest therapeutically active substances known to man."

As with needle exchange and methadone treatment, American politicians have ignored or spurned the findings of government commissions and scientific organizations concerning marijuana policy. In 1972 the National Commission on Marihuana and Drug Abuse—created by President Nixon and chaired by a former Republican governor, Raymond Shafer—recommended that possession of up to one ounce of marijuana be decriminalized. Nixon rejected the recommendation. In 1982 a panel appointed by the National Academy of Sciences reached the same conclusion as the Shafer Commission.

Between 1973 and 1978, with attitudes changing, 11 states approved decriminalization statutes that reclassified marijuana possession as a misdemeanor, petty offense, or civil violation punishable by no more than a $100 fine. Consumption trends in those states and in states that retained stricter sanctions were indistinguishable. A 1988 scholarly evaluation of the Moscone Act, California's 1976 decriminalization law, estimated that the state had saved half a billion dollars in arrest costs since the law's passage. Nonetheless, public opinion began to shift in 1978. No other states decriminalized marijuana, and some eventually recriminalized it.

Between 1973 and 1989, annual arrests on marijuana charges by state and local police ranged between 360,000 and 460,000. The annual total fell to 283,700 in 1991, but has since more than doubled. In 1996, 641,642 p   le were arrested for marijuana, 85% of them for possession, not   e, of the drug. Prompted by concern over rising marijuana use among adolescents and fears of being labeled soft on drugs, the Clinton administration launched its own anti-marijuana campaign in 1995. But the administration's claims to have identified new risks of marijuana consumption—including a purported link between marijuana and violent behavior—have not withstood scrutiny.[1] Neither Congress nor the White House seems likely to put the issue of marijuana policy before a truly independent advisory commission, given the consistency with which such commissions have reached politically unacceptable conclusions.

In contrast, governments in Europe and Australia, notably in the Netherlands, have reconsidered their cannabis policies. In 1976 the Baan Commission in the Netherlands recommended, and the Dutch government adopted, a policy of separating the "soft" and "hard" drug markets. Criminal penalties for and police efforts against heroin trafficking were increased, while those against cannabis were relaxed. Marijuana and hashish can now be bought in hundreds of "coffee shops" throughout the country. Advertising, open displays, and sales to minors are prohibited. Police quickly close coffee shops caught selling hard drugs. Almost no one is arrested or even fined for cannabis possession, and the government collects taxes on the gray market sales.

In the Netherlands today, cannabis consumption for most age groups is similar to that in the United States. Young Dutch teenagers, however, are less likely to sample marijuana than their American peers; from 1992 to 1994, only 7.2% of Dutch youths between the ages of 12 and 15 reported having tried marijuana, compared to 13.5% of Americans in that age bracket. Far fewer Dutch youths, moreover, experiment with cocaine, buttressing officials' claims of success in separating the markets for hard and soft drugs. Most Dutch parents regard the "reefer madness" anti-marijuana campaigns of the United States as silly.

Dutch coffee shops have not been problem free. Many citizens have complained about the proliferation of coffee shops, as well as nuisances created by foreign youth flocking to party in Dutch border cities. Organized crime involvement in the growing domestic cannabis industry is of increasing concern. The Dutch government's efforts to address the problem by more openly and systematically regulating supplies to coffee shops, along with some of its other drug policy initiatives, have run up against pressure from abroad, notably from Paris, Stockholm, Bonn, and Washington. In late 1995 French President Jacques Chirac began publicly berating The Hague for its drug policies, even threatening to suspend implementation of the Schengen Agreement allowing the free movement of people across borders of European Union (EU) countries. Some of Chirac's political allies called the Netherlands a narco-state. Dutch officials responded with evidence of the relative success of their policies, while pointing out that most cannabis seized in France originates in Morocco (which Chirac has refrained from criticizing because of his government's close relations with King Hassan). The Hague, however, did announce reductions in the number of coffee shops and the amount of cannabis customers can buy there. But it still sanctions the coffee shops, and a few municipalities actually operate them.

Notwithstanding the attacks, in the 1990s the trend toward decriminalization of cannabis has accelerated in Europe. Across much of western Europe, possession and even minor sales of the drug are effectively decriminalized. Spain decriminalized private use of cannabis in 1983. In Germany, the Federal Constitutional Court effectively sanctioned a cautious liberalization of cannabis policy in a widely publicized 1994 decision. German states vary considerably in their attitude; some, like Bavaria, persist in a highly punitive policy, but most now favor the Dutch approach. So far the Kohl administration has refused to approve state proposals to legalize and regulate cannabis sales, but it appears aware of the rising support in the country for Dutch and Swiss approaches to local drug problems.

In June 1996 Luxembourg's parliament voted to decriminalize cannabis and push for standardization of drug laws in the Benelux countries. The Belgian government is now considering a more modest decriminalization of cannabis combined with tougher measures against organized crime and heroin traffickers. In Australia, cannabis has been decriminalized in South Australia, the Australian Capital Territory (Canberra), and the Northern Territory, and other states are considering the step. Even in France, Chirac's outburst followed recommendations of cannabis decriminalization by three distinguished national commissions. Chirac must now contend with a new prime minister, Lionel Jospin, who declared himself in favor of decriminalization before his Socialist Party won the 1997 parliamentary elections. Public opinion is clearly shifting. A recent poll found that 51% of Canadians favor decriminalizing marijuana.

Will It Work?

Both at home and abroad, the U.S. government has attempted to block resolutions supporting harm reduction, suppress scientific studies that reached politically inconvenient conclusions, and silence critics of official drug policy. In May 1994 the State Department forced the last-minute cancellation of a World Bank conference on drug trafficking to which critics of U.S. drug policy had been invited. That December the U.S. delegation to an international meeting of the U.N. Drug Control Program refused to sign any statement incorporating the phrase "harm reduction." In early 1995 the State Department successfully pressured the World Health Organization to scuttle the release of a report it had commissioned from a panel that included many of the world's leading experts on cocaine because it included the scientifically incontrovertible observations that traditional use of coca leaf in the Andes causes little harm to users and that most consumers of cocaine use the drug in moderation with few detrimental effects. Hundreds of congressional hearings have addressed multitudinous aspects of the drug problem, but few have inquired into the European harm-reduction policies described above. When former Secretary of State George Shultz, then-Surgeon General M. Joycelyn Elders, and Baltimore Mayor Kurt Schmoke pointed to the failure of current policies and called for new approaches, they were mocked, fired, and ignored, respectively—and thereafter mischaracterized as advocating the outright legalization of drugs.

In Europe, in contrast, informed, public debate about drug policy is increasingly common in government, even at the EU level. In June 1995 the European Parliament issued a report acknowledging that "there will always be a demand for drugs in our societies . . . the policies followed so far have not been able to prevent the illegal drug trade from flourishing." The EU called for serious consideration of the Frankfurt Resolution, a statement of harm-reduction principles supported by a transnational coalition of 31 cities and regions. In October 1996 Emma Bonino, the European commissioner for consumer policy, advocated decriminalizing soft drugs and initiating a broad prescription program for hard drugs. Greece's minister for European affairs, George Papandreou, seconded her. In February 1997, the monarch of Liechtenstein, Prince Hans Adam, spoke out in favor of controlled drug legalization. Even Raymond Kendall, secretary general of Interpol, was quoted in the August 20, 1994, *Guardian* as saying, "The prosecution of thousands of otherwise law-abiding citizens every year is both hypocritical and an affront to individual, civil and human rights. . . . Drug use should no longer be a criminal offense. I am totally against legalization, but in favor of decriminalization for the user."

One can, of course, exaggerate the differences between attitudes in the United States and those in Europe and Australia. Many European leaders still echo Chirac's U.S. style anti-drug pronouncements. Most capital cities endorse the Stockholm Resolution, a statement backing punitive prohibitionist policies that was drafted in response to the Frankfurt Resolution. And the Dutch have had to struggle against French and other efforts to standardize more punitive drug laws and policies within the EU.

Conversely, support for harm-reduction approaches is growing in the United States, notably and vocally among public health professionals but also, more discreetly, among urban politicians and police officials. Some of the world's most innovative needle exchange and other harm-reduction programs can be found in America. The 1996 victories at the polls for California's Proposition 215, which legalizes the medicinal use of marijuana, and Arizona's Proposition 200, which allows doctors to prescribe any drug they deem appropriate and mandates treatment rather than jail for those arrested for possession, suggest that Americans are more receptive to drug policy reform than politicians acknowledge.

But Europe and Australia are generally ahead of the United States in their willingness to discuss openly and experiment pragmatically with alternative policies that might reduce the harm to both addicts and society. Public health officials in many European cities work closely with police, politicians, private physicians, and others to coordinate efforts. Community policing treats drug dealers and users as elements of the community that need not be expelled but can be made less troublesome. Such efforts, including crackdowns on open drug scenes in Zurich, Bern, and Frankfurt, are devised and implemented in tandem with initiatives to address health and housing problems. In the United States, in contrast, politicians presented with new approaches do not ask, "Will they work?" but only, "Are they tough enough?" Many legislators are reluctant to support drug treatment programs that are not punitive, coercive, and prison-based, and many criminal justice officials still view prison as a quick and easy solution for drug problems.

The lessons from Europe and Australia are compelling. Drug control policies should focus on reducing drug-related crime, disease, and death, not the number of casual drug users. Stopping the spread of HIV by and among drug users by making sterile syringes and methadone readily available must be the first priority. American politicians need to explore, not ignore or automatically condemn, promising policy options such as cannabis decriminalization, heroin prescription, and the integration of harm-reduction principles into community policing strategies. Central governments must back, or at least not hinder, the efforts of municipal officials and citizens to devise pragmatic approaches to local drug problems. Like citizens in Europe, the American public has supported such innovations when they are adequately explained and allowed to prove themselves. As the evidence comes in, what works is increasingly apparent. All that remains is mustering the political courage.

▇ Note

1. Zimmer, L., & Morgan, J. P. (1997). *Marijuana myths, marijuana facts: A review of the scientific evidence.* New York: Lindesmith Center.

Index

Accidents, 38
Adolescents, 16
   alcohol use, 13, 33-34, 35, 91, 144
   amphetamine use, 15
   cocaine use, 15
   crack business, 57
   daily drug use, 70
   decriminalization and, 39
   education of, 46
   increased drug use, 2, 23, 36, 158
   legalization/regulation approach and, 33
   marijuana use, 4, 9, 13, 14, 15, 17, 43,
     76, 85-86, 87, 90, 92, 93, 94, 155
   percent using drugs, 39
   tobacco use, 4, 10, 13, 17, 33-34, 35, 43,
     44, 45, 144
   See also specific drugs
Adversarial approach to treatment, 28

Advertising, 26
   alcohol, 137-138
   decriminalization and, 39, 45
   legalization/regulation approach and, 34
   tobacco, 46, 128, 137-138
African American(s), racist legal penalties
   and, 23, 133-136
African American males, working, 41
Age of first use, 39, 94
Aggression, drug effects and, 59-60
AIDS, *see* HIV/AIDS-related interventions
Alcohol, 159
   advertising, 137-138
   driving under the influence of, 62, 70
   drug policy and, 126, 131
   regulating, 21, 33-34, 35, 70,
     129-130
   War on Drugs and, 144-145

Alcohol use/abuse:
  adolescents, 13, 33-34, 35, 91, 144
  cost to society, 91
  dependence symptoms, 85
  gateway effect, 131, 140, 146
  health effects, 129
  marijuana and, 86, 91, 94
  number of users, 127
  prohibition and, 70, 88-89, 140, 142
  public opinion, 89
  risk perceptions, 77
  suicides and, 136
  treatment, 28
  universality of, 3
  using other drugs with, 155
  victims of violence using, 62, 68
  violence and, 60-61, 66, 145
American Bar Association, 30, 162
American drug experience, 2-4
American Medical Association, 11, 21, 30,
  162
Amphetamines, 15, 159
Analgesics, psychedelic revolution and, 4
Antabuse, 28
Arizona, medical use of marijuana and,
  29-30, 77
Armed robberies, 62
Arrest(s), 13, 91
Arrestees, drug use by, 16, 17, 23, 43, 153
Attention deficit/hyperactivity disorder,
  marijuana use and, 86
Autopsies, presence of marijuana in, 87, 92

Baby boomers, drug use and, 13, 94
Bauer, Gary, 144
Bennett, William, 21-22, 112, 118
Besteman, Karst J., 151-156
Bleach distribution, 6, 47
Buprenorphine, treating heroin addicts with,
  165
Bush administration, War on Drugs and,
  118, 138

California, medical use of marijuana and,
  29-30, 77
Cigarettes, see Tobacco
Civil rights, erosion of, 10, 12, 23, 24, 32,
  34, 36

Clinton administration, drug law violations
  in, 22
Coast Guard, 4
Coca:
  chewing, 3
  plant, 159
Cocaine:
  adolescents using, 15
  arrestees using, 16, 23, 43
  dependence symptoms, 85
  discovery of, 3
  driving under the influence of, 62
  high school seniors using, 70
  homicides and, 65, 66
  number of users, 128
  prices, 17, 63, 64
  purity of, 17
  seizures of, 16-17
  supply, 17, 128
  systemic violence and, 65
  victims of violence using, 61, 65-66, 68
  violence and, 58, 65, 68
  See also Crack cocaine; Powder cocaine
Cocaine psychosis, 58-59
Codeine, treating heroin addicts with, 165
Cognitive dissonance, War on Drugs and,
  130-131, 136-140
Commercialism, drug policy and, 11
Community policing strategies, 160
Condom distribution, 6, 25, 26, 122
Consciousness, drive to alter, 69
Consequentialist-legalizers, 114, 116
Consequentialist-prohibitionists, 114-115
Constitutional rights, 10
Consumerism policy, 37
Controlled Substances Act of 1970, 90
Courts:
  costs, 91
  drug, 23, 25, 91
  money spent on, 90
  racist, 23
  overwhelmed, 23, 34
Crack cocaine:
  crime and, 1
  crime and, 63-64
  epidemic, 4, 158
  homicides and, 66, 68-69
  legalization of, 57-58
  price of, 64
  violence and, 66, 68-69

Crack houses, 59
Crime, 5, 12, 16
    baby boomers and, 13
    crack cocaine and, 1
    current policy contributing to, 23
    decreasing rates, 22
    drug prices and, 63
    escalation of, 153
    heroin use and, 143
    legalization and, 34, 55-71, 113
    marijuana and, 59, 86
    methadone treatment and, 165
    prohibitionist views, 20
Criminal careers, 63, 68
Criminal justice system:
    corruption, 16, 23, 153
    costs associated with, 91, 92, 96, 166
    decriminalization policy and, 38
    harm reduction approach and, 24-25
    medical models and, 28
    overwhelmed, 23, 32, 34, 36
    prohibitionist approach, 20
    racial discrepancies, 23, 42, 44, 126,
        133-136
    War on Drugs and, 158
Criminal penalties, 4, 6. *See also* Sentencing
Crops:
    hemp, 76, 81-84, 92-93
    international, 5, 120, 126, 159
    substitution programs, 159
Culture:
    national drug, 136-137
    prohibitionist views, 19
Customs, 4

Dead zones, 57
Decriminalization, 6, 18, 19, 35-40, 91
    criticisms of, 38-39
    economic issues and, 40-41
    law enforcement efforts, 133
    legalization and, 57, 113
    marijuana, 14, 90, 93, 94, 160
    social support for, 45
    violence and, 64
    War on Drugs and, 129-130
Demand, 4, 46
    drug prices and, 91
    failure to reduce, 23
    hemp, 83, 84

legalization and, 33, 69
marijuana, 91
prohibitionist approach, 20
reducing, 159
Dennis, Michael L., 75-97
Designer drugs, 4
Deterrence, 153
    absolute versus relative, 117-119
    classic model, 4
    failure of, 44, 117
    limited effect of, 33
    prohibitionist views, 19
    relative, 19
Disease, drug abuse as, 27-28
Distribution:
    legalization/regulation and, 33-34, 35, 45
    medical profession and, 11
Diversion programs, 14-15, 25, 46, 122
Dope fiends, 12
Drinking age, 70
Drive-by shootings, 67
Driving while under the influence, 62, 70,
    92, 152
Dronabinol, 30
Drug abuse, *see* Drug use/abuse
Drug analysis units, 160
Drug courts, 23, 25, 91
Drug culture, national, 136-137
Drug dealers:
    demonization of, 139
    gun ownership, 67
    legalization approach and, 33-34
    lower class and, 41
    marijuana use and, 86
    profit motive, 16, 33, 35, 42, 117-118
    urban areas, 5, 16
    using drugs, 62
    violence and, 67, 69, 152
    War on Drugs and, 151
    youth, 57
Drug demand, *see* Demand
Drug effects, aggression and, 59-60
Drug Enforcement Administration, 4, 30, 164
Drug policies, 1-7
    alternative perspectives on, 9-49
    baby boomers and, 13-15
    basis of, 114-117
    commonsense, 157-172
    continuum today, 18-40
    data and, 140-144, 153-154

decriminalization, *see* Decriminalization
economy and, 40-43, 47-49
effective, 140
failure of, 44, 117, 125-147, 157-158
failure of War on Drugs, 117, 125-147
fallacies, 111
harm reduction approach, *see* Harm
  reduction approach
history of, 11-15, 112-114
legalization/regulation, 18, 19, 32-35
medicalization, *see* Medicalization
medical marijuana, 29-32, 80-81,
  101-108, 140-141
medical models, 27-29
middle ground, 121-124
modern debate, 15-18
prohibition, 18, 19-22
punitive, 14-15
Reagan administration and, 9, 15, 112,
  118
reform movement, 145-147
theory and, 47
unanticipated consequences, 119-121
zero tolerance, 9, 12, 15, 16, 26, 153
Drug prices:
  cocaine, 17
  crime and, 63, 64
  demand and, 91
  legalization and, 113
  marijuana, 102
  prohibition and, 102
Drug supply, *see* Supply
Drug tests, 44, 152-153
Drug traffickers/trafficking, 3, 137
  corruption caused by, 153
  effect of, 159
  profits for, 16, 159
  setting example of, 4
  systemic violence and, 65
  War on Drugs and, 151
Drug use/abuse, 1
  alcohol use with, 155
  adolescent, 13, 14, 16, 17, 39
  as disease, 27-28
  attitudes abroad, 159-161
  availability and, 141-142
  baby boomers and, 13, 94
  containing, 118
  crime and, *see* Crime
  driving under the influence and, 62, 152

free choice and, 39
glamorizing, 1-2, 136
high school students, 15
historical context, 2-3
increased adolescent, 2, 23, 36, 158
managing, 6
1980s, 158
1990s patterns, 17-18
recreational, 70
safe, 26
society's attitude toward, 15-16
See also specific drugs
Drug users:
  input from, 157
  teaching safer practices, 47
Drug war, *see* War on Drugs
DuPont, Robert, 14

Economically compulsive violence, 62-64,
  68
Economic development, 26, 46-47
Economic issues:
  drug policy and, 40-43
  hemp and, 81-84
Economic opportunities, 40, 48
Economy:
  drug policy and, 47-49
  legitimate, 11
Ecstasy, 160
Ecstasy, 4
Education, 4, 5
  harm reduction approach, 24, 25, 46, 122
  legalization/regulation approach and, 33
  opportunities, 40
  prohibitionist approach, 22
  public health approach, 155
Employment:
  assistance, 24
  drug testing for, 152-153
  lower class and, 41
  marijuana dependence, 92
  methadone treatment and, 166
  minorities, 42-43
  opportunities, 40
  suburban, 41
Employment-related problems, 20
Enslavement theory, 63
Europe, public debate about drug policy in
  170

Family dysfunction, 152
Family structure, disruption of, 20
Fashion industry, heroin chic and, 2
Federal government:
    drug abuse control, 4
    medical marijuana and, 30
    methadone support, 25
Female gang members, 41-42
Films, *see* Movies
Firearm violence, 66-67
Foreign policy, 5, 16
Free choice, right to, 37, 39
Free market approach, 36-38, 39, 40, 41,
    45-46
Friedman, Milton, 113
Funding, for education and prevention, 46

Gangs, 5, 16
    crack and, 57
    drug selling, 41, 42
    violence and, 67-68
Gates, Darryl, 21, 112-113
Gateway effect, 30, 80, 84, 87, 131, 140, 146
Global economy, 47
Global hemp market, 83
Goldstein, Paul J., 58
Goode, Erich, 18, 111-124
Government:
    legalization/regulation approach and,
        32-35
    regulation failure, 36-38
Grinspoon, Lester, 101-108
Guns, 43
    drug involvement, 66-67
    libertarians and, 145
    suicide committed using, 136

Hagedorn, J., 41-43, 48
Hallucinogens, 70, 159
Harm, definition of, 27
Harm reduction approach, 10, 24-27,
    159-172
    as middle ground, 18, 111-112, 121-124
    decriminalization and, 36
    economic development and, 46-47
    economic issues and, 40
    legalization and, 6, 33
    marijuana and, 167-170

Harrison Narcotics Act of 1914, 3, 4, 12, 112
Hashish, psychedelic revolution and, 4
Hawkins, Gordon, 119
Health care costs, 38, 166
Health issues, 129, 139, 145
    legalization/regulation approach and, 34
    marijuana, 91-92
Hemp crops, 76, 81-84, 92-93
Hemp Taxation Act of 1933, 83
Heroin:
    discovery of, 3
    legalization of, 90-91
    movement to mainstream culture, 1-2, 4
    popularity of, 4
    prices, 63
    violence and, 65
    War on Drugs and, 139, 151
Heroin chic, 2
Heroin use:
    crime and, 143
    high school seniors, 70
    inner cities, 4
    treatment, 28, 45, 122, 160, 163-167
Hispanics:
    War on Drugs and, 133
    working males, 41
HIV/AIDS-related interventions, 6, 24, 26,
    32, 143-144, 161-163
HIV infection, 13, 20, 23
Homicides, 59, 152
    alcohol use, 60-61, 62, 66
    cocaine use and, 65, 66
    crack and, 57
    gang-related, 67

Idealist-legalization position, 115
Incarceration:
    costs of, 46, 90
    nonwhites, 133
    number of people, 158
    treatment and, 47
Inciardi, James A., 1-7, 9-49, 55-71
Individual rights, societal rights versus, 80
Inhalants, 2, 70, 159
Inhibitions, drugs and alcohol reducing, 59,
    60
Initiation, age of, 39, 94
Inner cities:
    crack and, 57

drug dealers, 5, 16
economic issues, 41-43
gang violence, 68
harm reduction approach, 27
heroin use, 4
poverty and, 41
systemic violence and, 65
violence in, 61-62, 65, 68
Interdiction, 4, 10
    failure of, 137, 142-143
    medical models, 28
    prohibitionist approach, 20
    Reagan administration and, 9, 15
    success of, 16-17
    War on Drugs and, 151
Interference approach to treatment, 28
International crops, 5, 120, 126, 159
International law and agreements, American
        drug policy and, 22
International law enforcement, 159
Interventions, 128
    ancillary, 7
    social context, 48
Islam, resurgent, 22

Jails:
    nonwhites in, 133
    overcrowded, 5, 16
Jobs, *see* Employment
Jonas, Steven, 125-147
"Just Say No," 15, 26, 32, 44, 94
Juvenile arrestees, drug tests and, 44

Kaplan, John, 118, 119
Kleiman, Mark, 122

Latinos, *see* Hispanics
Law(s):
    draconian, 15, 22, 23
    drug policy role, 47
    history of, 3
    1980s, 90
    paraphernalia, 6, 162
Law enforcement, 4
    corruption, 5, 16, 23, 153
    costs, 90, 91, 113
    deterrence and, 117-118

drug policy role, 47
international, 159
marijuana and, 88
1950s, 13
prohibitionist approach, 19-20
public health approach and, 154-155
public support for, 36
racist, 23, 133-136
War on Drugs and, 151
Legalization, 2, 5-7
    baby boomers and, 13-14
    costs of, 90-92
    crack cocaine, 57-58
    crime and, 68, 113
    decriminalization and, 57, 113
    demand and, 69
    drug prices and, 113
    drug use rates and, 118-119
    framework, 18
    hemp, 81-84
    marijuana, 10, 14, 21, 23, 34, 75-97
    medicalization and, 56-57, 113
    medical marijuana and, 29-32, 80-81
    politically unwise, 160
    prohibitionist views, 20-21
    public opinion and, 21, 32
    societal consequences, 33
    systemic violence and, 65
    true, 56
    unanticipated consequences, 120
    violent crime and, 55-71
Legalization/regulation approach, 18, 19,
        32-35
    critics of, 34-35
    decriminalization and, 36
    economic issues and, 40
    physicians and, 45
Legislation, 4, 5, 89-90
Levomethadyl acetate hydrochloride, 28
Libertarian issues, 37, 93, 113, 145
Lindesmith, Alfred R., 12
Living expenses, crime paying for, 63-64
Local level, social action at, 48
LSD:
    psychedelic revolution and, 4
    recent increase in youth using, 2

Maintenance models of treatment, 28
Mandatory sentencing, 15, 22

Marijuana:
    adolescents using, 4, 9-10, 13, 14, 15, 17,
       76, 85, 87, 90, 92, 93, 94, 155
    alcohol use and, 86, 91, 94
    commercial uses, 76, 81-84, 92-93
    consequences of use, 84-87
    costs to society, 90-92, 93
    decriminalization of, 14, 90, 160
    dependence, 85, 87, 92, 93
    driving under the influence of, 62, 92
    effectiveness of regulations, 88-90
    gateway effect, 30, 80, 84, 87
    harm reduction approach, 167-170
    health consequences of, 91-92
    increased worldwide production of, 17
    indigenous, 3
    legalization of, 10, 14, 21, 23, 34, 75-97
    medical, 29-32, 43, 80-81, 92, 96,
       101-108
    percent of users, 77, 94
    price of, 102
    psychedelic revolution and, 4
    recent increase in use, 2, 4, 89-90
    right to use, 77-80
    risk perceptions, 17-18, 43, 77, 88, 94, 96
    seizures of, 16-17
    tobacco use and, 94
    violence and, 59-60, 91
Marijuana Tax Act of 1937, 75, 102
Marinol, 30
McBride, Duane C., 9-49
McCaffrey, Barry, 139, 140 141
McWilliams, Peter, 116
Media:
    anti-drug messages, 2
    drug abuse stories, 1
    drug-oriented popular, 14
    drug user portrayal by, 13
Medical condition, drug abuse as, 23
Medical marijuana, 29-32, 43, 80-81, 92, 96,
      101-108, 140-141
Medical models:
    of drug policy reform, 27-29
    economic issues and, 40
Medicalization, 12, 18, 19, 33, 44-45, 56-57,
    113
Mental health perspective, 14-15
Methadone maintenance, 25, 28, 45, 160,
    163-167
Methamphetamine, violent behavior and, 58

Mill, John Stuart, 36, 38
Minorities:
    drug use by, 43-44
    employment, 42-43
    legalization harming, 20
    racist legal penalties, 23, 133-136
    War on Drugs and, 125, 126, 133-136,
      138
Moralist(s), 160
Moralist-legalization position, 115-116
Moralist-prohibitionist position, 115
Moral reformers, 11, 19
Moral weight, of saving lives, 123
Morphine:
    discovery of, 3
    treating heroin addicts with, 165
Mothers, crack-addicted, 57
Movies, heroin's popularity and, 2
Muggings, 62

Nadelmann, Ethan A., 117-118, 121, 157-172
Narcotic Addict Rehabilitation Act, 14
National Institute on Drug Abuse, 14
National Organization for Reform of
    Marijuana Laws, 14
Needle(s), invention of, 3
Needle distribution, 6, 23, 25, 26
Needle exchange programs, 27, 46, 122,
    143-144, 161-162
Netherlands:
    heroin treatment, 166
    legalization in, 34
    needle exchange, 161
Nicotine addicts, 70
Nixon, Richard M., 151
Nixon administration, War on Drugs and, 9

Offenders, mandatory treatment for, 2
Office of National Drug Control Policy, 22
Opium:
    1800s use, 11
    growing, 159
    increased worldwide production of, 17
    international production, 120
    medicinal use, 3
Opium poppy, indigenous, 3
Overdoses, 136
Over-the-counter drugs, 3, 137

Palfium, treating heroin addicts with, 165
Paraphernalia:
    decriminalization and, 36
    laws, 6, 162
PCP, 4
Perinatal transmission, 23
Pharmaceutical industry, 145
Pharmacotherapeutic treatment, 28
Phoenix, River, 2
Physicians:
    control of illicit substances, 28, 45
    medical marijuana and, 29-32
    methadone treatment, 164-165
    treatment and, 160
Policies, see Drug policies
Poor, legalization harming, 20
Poverty, inner cities and, 41
Powder cocaine:
    crack manufactured from, 58
    current use of, 4
Prescription drugs, 130, 145, 155
Prevention, 4
    harm reduction approach, 24, 26-27, 46
    marijuana and, 88
    1980s, 90
    prohibitionist approach, 20
    public health approach, 155
Prisons:
    costs, 90, 91
    needle exchange, 161
    nonwhites in, 133
    overcrowded, 34
Probation, 47
Prohibition approach, 10, 114
    alcohol and, 70, 88-89, 140, 142
    corruption effects, 44
    costs of, 90-92
    critics of, 22-24, 32
    current policy of, 18, 19-22
    deterrence and, 117
    drug prices and, 102
    economic issues and, 40
    effectiveness of, 88-89
    failure of, 160
    limited success of, 16
    public opinion on, 93
Property crimes, 62
Prostitution, 62
Psychedelic revolution, 1960s, 4
Psychoactive plants, 3

Psychopharmacological violence, 58-62,
        65-66, 68
Public health:
    consequences of drug use, 32
    goals, 160
    harm reduction approach, 23, 25
    legalization/regulation approach and, 34
    prohibition and, 40
Public health perspective, 12, 23, 146-147,
        153-156
Public health reformers, 11
Public opinion:
    alcohol use and, 89
    legalization and, 21, 32, 89-90, 96
    marijuana legalization, 96
    needle exchange, 162
    prohibition, 93
Public support, for law enforcement, 36
Punishment:
    limited success of, 16
    rational choice theory and, 12
    severity and certainty of, 21-22, 33, 153
    War on Drugs and, 125
Punitive approach, 10, 12, 14, 112
    deterrence and, 117
    failure of, 44, 117
    moderate, 117
    prohibition and, 19, 20
    Reagan era, 15
    unanticipated consequences, 120
Pure Food and Drug Act of 1906, 3

Quaaludes, 4

Race:
    criminal justice system and, 23, 42, 44,
        126, 133-136
    disparate legal penalties and, 23, 133-136
    War on Drugs and, 125, 126, 130,
        132-136
Rational choice:
    drug use and, 41
    punishment and, 12
Rational consumers, legalization/regulation
        approach and, 33
Reagan administration, drug policy and, 9,
        15, 112, 118
Recidivism, harm reduction approach and,
        25

Reform era, 1800s, 11-13, 19
Regulation:
  expectation of, 38, 45
  failure of, 36-38
  see Legalization/regulation
Reno, Janet, 22
Reuter, Peter, 121
Rituals, drugs used in, 3
Rock groups, heroin use by, 1-2
Role models, 26
Room, Robin, 95

Safe injection rooms, 160, 167
Schmoke, Kurt L., 5, 34
School problems, 20
Searches and seizures, 126
Sedatives:
  high school seniors using, 70
  psychedelic revolution and, 4
Sentencing:
  mandatory, 15, 22
  marijuana users, 96
  racist, 126, 133
Sexually transmitted diseases, 6
Sin tax, 90
Social action, at local level, 48
Social context, of interventions, 48
Social policies, intractable problems and, 95
Social reform, 11, 19, 95
Social structural changes, 47-48
Societal aid, expectation of, 38, 45
Societal consequences, of legalization, 33
Societal problems, 71
Societal rights, individual rights versus, 80
Society:
  alcohol's costs to, 91
  attitude toward drug use, 15-16
  costs of marijuana to, 90-92, 93, 96
  dysfunctional aspects, 69
  free and democratic, 37
  harm to, 122
  immoral behavior and, 115
Sociocultural institutions, breakdown of, 68
Solvents, 159
States, medical use of marijuana and, 29-30
Stimulants:
  psychedelic revolution and, 4
  recent increase in youth using, 2
  violent behavior and, 58

Suburbs, jobs moving to, 41
Suicides, 136
Supply, 4
  cocaine, 17
  drug use and, 141-142
  futility of reducing, 159
  prohibitionist approach, 20
  reducing, 55
  War on Drugs and, 125, 127-128, 130
Switzerland:
  heroin treatment, 165-166
  legalization in, 34, 143
  safe-injection rooms, 166
Syringe distribution, 6, 23, 143-144, 160,
    161-163
Systemic violence, 65-69, 71
Szasz, Thomas, 35, 37, 38, 113

Terry, Yvonne M., 9-49
THC, 30, 80, 81, 83, 84, 87, 93, 104, 105,
    106, 141
Tobacco, 159
  adolescents using, 4, 10, 13, 17, 33, 35,
    43, 44, 45, 144
  advertising, 46, 128, 137-138
  decline in use, 146-147
  dependence symptoms, 85
  drug policy, 131
  gateway effect, 131, 140, 146
  gross yield, 82-83
  health effects, 129, 139, 145
  marijuana use and, 94
  number of users, 127
  peak consumption, 141
  policy needs and, 126
  recent increase in youth using, 2, 4
  regulating, 21, 33-34, 35, 44, 129-130
  War on Drugs and, 144-145
Treatment, 4
  availability of, 163-164
  broader options, 6
  decriminalization and, 36
  dependence symptoms and, 85
  diversion into, 14-15, 25, 46, 122
  effectiveness of, 15, 25, 27, 46
  harm reduction approach, 24, 25, 46, 122
  heroin use, 28, 45, 160, 163-167
  incarceration and, 47
  legalization and, 90

marijuana and, 88, 93
medical models, 28, 45
needle exchange referrals, 144
number of slots, 5
offenders, 2
physicians and, 160
prohibitionist approach, 20, 22
retention, 15
utilization, 15
War on Drugs and, 10, 151
Treatment Alternatives to Street Crime
        (TASC), 25, 46
Treatment-on-demand, 29
Trebach, Arnold S., 37, 57, 120

Unanticipated consequences, of drug
        policies, 119-121
Urban areas, *see* Inner cities
Urban sociology, 48

Victims of violence, alcohol/drug use by,
        61-62, 65-66, 68
Violence, 38
    alcohol use and, 60-61, 66, 145
    crack cocaine and, 1
    decriminalization and, 64
    drug dealers and, 152

economically compulsive, 62-64, 68
    indirect, 66
    legalization effects, 55-71, 90
    marijuana and, 59-60, 91
    psychopharmacological, 58-62, 65-66, 68
    systemic, 65-69, 71
    War on Drugs and, 129
Vitamins, 137

War on Drugs, 4-5, 15, 55
    effectiveness of, 118
    expenditures for, 16, 158
    failure of, 117, 125-147
    futility of, 6
    history of, 9, 112, 151
Welfare reform, 42
White, William, 75-97
Whites:
    criminal justice system and, 42
    drug use by, 44, 133, 146
    male gang members, working, 41
Wilson, James Q., 22, 115
Withdrawal, 28, 59

Zero tolerance, 9, 12, 15, 16, 26, 153
Zimring, Franklin, 119

About the Contributors

Karst J. Besteman, M.S.W., is former deputy director of the National Institute on Drug Abuse and Assistant Surgeon General, PHS (Ret.). He participated in the implementation of federal drug abuse demand reduction programs from 1957 through 1980. He has served as executive director of the Alcohol and Drug Problems Association where he focused on advocating for effective public policy to solve the problems of substance abuse. He has carried out research in treatment effectiveness and presently serves as Chief Executive Officer of CMAC, Inc. which operates substance abuse treatment programs.

Michael L. Dennis, Ph.D., is a senior research psychologist in the Lighthouse Institute of Chestnut Health Systems, a methodologist, and Principal Investigator of the SAMHSA/CSAT's Cannabis Youth Treatment Cooperative Agreement Study.

Erich Goode, Ph.D., is currently Professor of Sociology at the State University of New York at Stony Brook. He has taught at Columbia, New York University, Florida Atlantic University, University of North Carolina at Chapel Hill, and Hebrew University of Jerusalem. His books include *The Marijuana Smokers* (1970), *Drugs in American Society* (5th ed. 1999), *Deviant Behavior* (5th ed. 1997), *Moral Panics* (with Nachman Ben-Yehuda, 1994), and *Between Politics and Reason: The Drug Legalization Debate* (1997). He was a contributor to the National Commission on Marihuana and Drug Abuse, *Marihuana: A Signal of Misunderstanding*, which shaped federal and state legal policy toward marijuana control in the 1970s. His current interests include autoethnography and the sociology of paranormal beliefs. He is recipient of a Guggenheim Fellowship.

Lester Grinspoon, M.D., is Associate Professor of Psychiatry at Harvard University Medical School. He is author of a number of books about drugs including the *Marihuana Reconsidered* and, with James B. Baklar, *Marihuana: The Forbidden Medicine*.

James A. Inciardi, Ph.D., is Director of the Center for Drug and Alcohol Studies at the University of Delaware, Professor in that university's Department of Sociology and Criminal Justice, Adjunct Professor in the Department of Epidemiology and Public Health at the University of Miami School of Medicine, Distinguished Professor at the State University of Rio de Janeiro, and a Guest Professor in the Department of Psychiatry at the Federal University of Rio Grande do Sul in Porto Alegre, Brazil. With 30 years of experience in the field of drug abuse, he has done extensive consulting work both nationally and internationally, and he has published more than 270 articles, chapters, books and monographs in the areas of substance abuse, criminology, criminal justice, history, folklore, social policy, AIDS, medicine, and law.

Steven Jonas, M.D., M.P.H., M.S., is Professor of Preventive Medicine at State University of New York at Stony Brook. He has authored 8 books of his own and has edited and coauthored another 10 on health policy, health promotion and disease prevention, and national politics, as well as over 100 professional articles and book reviews and numerous popular articles. Since 1989, he has published over 10 papers and book/monograph chapters on national recreational drug policy in such venues as *American Behavioral Scientist, Hofstra Law Review, American Journal of Health Promotion, Preventive Medicine, Connecticut Law Review,* and the textbook *Substance Abuse.* His drug policy work has focused primarily on the U.S. Drug Culture, the Public Health Approach to the Drug Problem, and the political economy of drug use and the drug war.

Duane C. McBride, Ph.D., is a sociologist and currently serves as Professor and Chair of the Behavioral Sciences Department at Andrews University, Administrative Director of that university's Institute for the Prevention of Addictions, and an Adjunct Professor in the Department of Epidemiology and Public Health at the University of Miami School of Medicine. He earned a Ph.D. in sociology (deviant behavior) from the University of Kentucky. He has been involved in substance abuse research for over 20 years and has published over 60 articles, monographs, and books in the areas of substance use, treatment program evaluation, and AIDS risk behaviors. He also chairs a grant review committee for the National Institute on Drug Abuse (NIDA) and is a frequent special reviewer for NIDA and other federal institutes. Currently, he is the Co-Principal Investigator for the Center for Health Services Research at the University of Miami School of Medicine.

Ethan A. Nadelmann, Ph.D., J.D., is Director of the Lindesmith Center, a drug policy research institute in New York, and author of *Cops Across Borders: The Internationalization of U.S. Criminal Law Enforcement* (1993). His writings on drug policy have appeared in numerous scholarly and mainstream journals and publications including *Science, National Review, Foreign Policy, Foreign Affairs, Daedalus, The Public Interest,* and *International Organization.* He is a highly regarded expert on the international aspects of crime and law enforcement. He has spoken directly to diverse audiences throughout the world and appeared on scores of radio and TV programs, including ABC's *Nightline,* BBC *Newsnight,* NBC *Nightly News,* and CNN's *Larry King Live.*

Yvonne M. Terry is currently completing a Master of Science degree in Administration at the University of Notre Dame and is a Research Associate for the Department of Behavioral Sciences at Andrews University. She is project director of a study examining trends and correlates in substance use in a adolescent population. She is author of a book on the interaction between religious mission and culture, and coauthor of a variety of articles on drug policy, evaluation of HIV risk-education programs, and gender voice in policy making. Her research areas include international development, public health, and youth drug use.

William White, M.A., is a senior consultant and trainer in the Lighthouse Institute of Chestnut Health Systems, a substance abuse treatment historian, and the cross-site clinical coordinator of the SAMHSA/CSAT's Cannabis Youth Treatment Cooperative Agreement Study.